A DEEP AND PERFECT VISION

Dhamma Talks by Ajahn Luang Por Tate
(Tate Taterangsee)

Translated in the Dhamma by Ajahn Sumano Bhikkhu

Ajahn Sumano Bhikkhu P.O. Box 3, Glang Dong
Nakorn Ratchisima 30320 Thailand

E-mail: monksumano@yahoo.com
Web site: www.next-life.com

Author   : Ajahn Sumano Bhikkhu
Translation   : Ajahn Sumano Bhikkhu
Publisher   : Double-Eyed Cave Meditation Sanctuary

Producer   : Gaangaew Punyaratabandhu

Senior Editor   : Alexander John Pithie,
                  alexpithie@gmail.com

Editors   : Fred Wieck, Greg Caroll,
                  Roy Harmic, Sumaet Punyaratabandu

Layout & Artwork   : Athapon Korapoom
Print Co-coordinator : Wanida Phadungphong
Printer   : LOL Ad House Co., Ltd.

DVD Production : Ron van Zelst

First edition   : July 2009,
5000 copies

ISBN 978-0-578-02307-6

Printed and produced in Thailand

Introduction

Ajahn Sumano Bhikkhu lives in the north east of Thailand. The serene, isolated cave sanctuary of which he is steward is a bio-diversity 'island.' Five thousand trees and varieties of native flora have been planted on and at the foot of the mountain he stewards. Over the past three years he worked on translating the teachings of several of the great wandering forest monks who hardly known outside of Thailand. Several days a month he receives visitors interested in meditation. Aside from these duties, he meditates and watches the seasons change.

The Double-Eyed Cave Sanctuary

I have chosen to live my monastic life in a peaceful, naturally balanced environment that allows for a kind of flexible solitude. I live in and around a mountain.

I have planted trees all over the mountain in order to create a diversified bio-environment for the long-term benefit of the nearby villages. Mostly, I practice formal meditation inside a cave, though I sometimes make use of a hut below where I work with an ancient laptop. The food I eat is mostly vegetarian (although I accept all offerings of food and money which I utilize to publish and distribute books.). Disciples and supporters bring me the things I need to live, i.e. soap, toothpaste, etc. Actually, most of the food I receive on alms rounds is sent off to agricultural workers picking fruits in the surrounding orchards. The remaining vegetables and fruits constitute most of my daily meal. I receive visitors and teach on week-ends. I see this way-place as one kind of spiritually-based environment. You too can live simply, with discipline and awareness, and create an equally effective environment for yourself.

Since I arrived in the forests of Northeast Thailand in the 1980s, dozens of Western monks have come and gone. A few are still here waiting for "the fat lady to sing." Most went back to the West with their Dhamma treasure. When many of them returned to the West, they move on with the "Heart" of the forest monks.

Ajahn Sumedho, Ajahn Geoff, Ajahn Amaro, Ajahn Jinavanso continue to seek their freedom through the monastic form of a Bhikkhu (world-ender). Paul Breiter,

Jack Kornfield, and dozens of others became householders and have boldly and confidently lived the householder's life, working, raising children, taking the garbage out, struggling with finances, leading retreats, keeping their marriages together, and staying on track.

While they were here, they learned that the body and mind are not personal, not really ours. These things and all other things change, one cannot expect to find much happiness in the world, and that the ego is an amalgamation of experiences, conditioning, karma, environmental influences and genes. And when it's all said and done, the happiness we do so passionately pursue is insubstantial and not worth the trouble we went through chasing after it all.

Deeply knowing these facts is the foundation for wisdom. This is the key that opens the door to freedom. The Teaching of the Buddha, stated succinctly, is that the catalyst for wisdom to arise comes from the knowing (Realizing), in the present moment, that all things are in a state of flux, all conditions are somewhere between mildly and desperately unsatisfactory, and that the idea of who we think we are is a deception (annata, no-self) based on ignorance.

This ignorance has dominated our life for years, for lifetimes while we cried "enough tears to fill all the oceans." We would be judicious to remember that the duty of ignorance is to conceal the Truth...and it possesses the power to do a magnificent job of it.

What brought me to the forest was the recognition that much of the approach to the Buddha-Dhamma that had been so effective in my practice in the United States actually came out of the forests here in Thailand. Earlier, I had practiced in the Zen and Tibetan traditions which had a romantic and exotic attraction that the forest tradition (Theravada) lacked. The venues for the retreats were always much more exhilarating than the no-nonsense setting and venues used by the Theravada teachers. When the choice was between a school dormitory in Indiana and a resort in Hawaii, I usually opted for the later. It was easy to overlook the efficacy of the simple, straightforward approach of developing mindfulness (sati) Vipassana that is central to the forest practice re-invigorated by Luang Por Mun.

Still, something deep inside me brought me to Southeast Asia and into the sphere of influence of the amazing old forest monks in "Amazing Thailand."

Those of you who have had some experience with meditation already know that the monastic tradition here in the Northeast has fertilized the Dhamma teaching in North America, Australia, and all of Europe. As an example of the extent of their impact, I was invited to lead a retreat in Russia in 1989. The entire group of participates were all committed Buddhists beginning back when they first encountered the teaching of the Buddha-Dhamma in their youth. Most were professors who had access to Buddhist books (such as Burmese and Thai translations) inaccessible to ordinary Russians. These men and women maintained a secret Buddhist meditation and study group throughout the era of the U.S.S.R.

By translating these talks in English I hope to fill a vacuum. Several Thai masters are now well-known in the West through translations and Web sites dedicated to their teaching. The three most familiar in the West are Ajahn

Cha, Ajahn Buddhadasa, and Ajahn Mahabooa. These highly revered teachers all had Western disciples who were able to translate and publish their talks into English during their lifetimes. However, Luang Por Tate (Ajahn Tate Rangsee) died before anyone could undertake an extensive project aimed at producing a book of this nature. Now, they are available to you.

Ajahn Tate's Teachings are worthy of our contemplation for their clarity and engaging imagery. All his efforts were solely aimed helping to remember, and to know, the cause of the delusion we embrace in our everyday, every-moment lives. We have thoroughly convinced ourselves that the show is the reality. As a Master of the Path, he compassionately illuminates The-Way-of-the-Buddhas which points us out from under the trance induced, conventional perception that drive our modern, distractive lifestyles. Supporting the deception are the pop gurus of the popular media who encourage us to continue shooting ourselves in the foot, anesthetizing our spiritual life while promoting unskillful living.

Using compelling imagery and analogies steeped in an ancient and fascinating heritage, he points toTruth while acknowledging the actual oneness of Truth when witnessed from different perspectives and practices.

Monks such as he started life as simple shepards tending water buffalos while they grazed in the rice fields and bathed in the village water hole. These were simple chores, yet required sufficient awareness and skillfulness to be able to respond to the herd's often sudden and unpredictable behavior. It was easy to be gored or trampled by these big creatures in a moment of carelessness or confusion. Water buffalo boys looking after the family's animals and rice fields grew up in a natural environment which supports maintaining a simple, ordinary mind that at the same time was intent, focused, and calm.

I know you will enjoy the unique flavor of the Forest-Dhamma. Back just fifty years ago tigers and elephants roamed freely, people believed that ghosts and spirits lurked behind every tree (superstition was rife), poisonous snakes, scorpions, and centipedes either killed people or disabled them for life. Their teaching analogies come out of farm life…rice plants, trees, water buffalos; scythe sharpening, cloth making, and the everyday encounters with reptiles and insects.

These pioneer forest monks lived all over these jungles. As little as fifty years ago, tigers and elephants roamed freely. People believed in ghosts and spirits to the extent that they regarded the jungle surrounding them as a fearful haven shielding all manner of scary creatures. The young monks had to overcome these attitudes. Actually, there didn't need to be ghosts or spirits behind every tree, there were plenty of poisonous snakes around and malaria was always a deadly factor in people's lives. However, the snakes and the malaria were not any where near as troublesome as the scorpions, centipedes, slender green vipers, biting ants, wasps, and super itchy caterpillars which can take you out for days. This is still true today, for if you're not well enough to get around, you are going to be incapable of getting food on alms round. The end result of infirmity is direct and certain.

Tough consequences such as these continually demand a wary and heedful state of attention. What's behind the door? What's sitting on the branch you're going to brush by? What's under that rock you may want to sit on? Mind you, that necessity for astute awareness is very much to the advantage of the sincere seeker.

We all need teachers to indicate the way. Therefore, the opportunity to contemplate on the-way-things-are is an opportunity not to be squandered. I believe these talks can do much to awaken the reader. The attentive reader will get a sense of how, over the course of countless lifetimes, ignorance has intensified and magnified to the point where we can go from day one to the moment of our death without even a single moment of awaken consciousness. We carry many false assumptions, in slavery to ignorance, about who we think we are life-time, after life-time, after life-time. It doesn't have to be this way.

Ajahn Sumano Bhikkhu

Double-Eyed Cave Sanctuary

Translator's Note

These talks took three years of sporadic work to complete. Ajahn Tate spoke in the Issan-Lao dialect which required astute listening and, as it turned out, high tech computer software to properly discern. The audio-tapes to be transcribed were very old, making the job even more challenging. There were many instances, for example, where background noises intruded, or someone up front had a coughing fit! While I have intentionally focused on these three talks, I listened to dozens of his talks over a period of 12 years and read everything available in Thai. The time spent listening and reading has been the foundation which gave me the courage ("gumlung jai" or strength) to undertake this delicate project.

I have been determined to see to it that my time and your time are best served. Therefore, I have presented Ajahn Tate's talks to communicate their essence rather than to publish a literal representation. And, I will at times elaborate to communicate the richness of the Buddha-Dhamma talks. I have occasionally contributed my understanding of critical points that the master intended to convey. A sensitive reader will appreciate the vividness and depth of these talks.

Before adding or expanding anything, I have reflected on each enhancement for hours until I felt confident I had something substantial to offer to better communicate an idea, point, or concept. I hope you can make the most out of this sublime opportunity. If what I was striving to communicate and share with you through a Deep and Perfect Vision, then all this will while for this translator as well as for the reader.

Remember this. Understanding the Path of Practice and then taking it to the final moment is something that can be done in a matter of months. You can end here.

Ajahn Sumano Bhikkhu

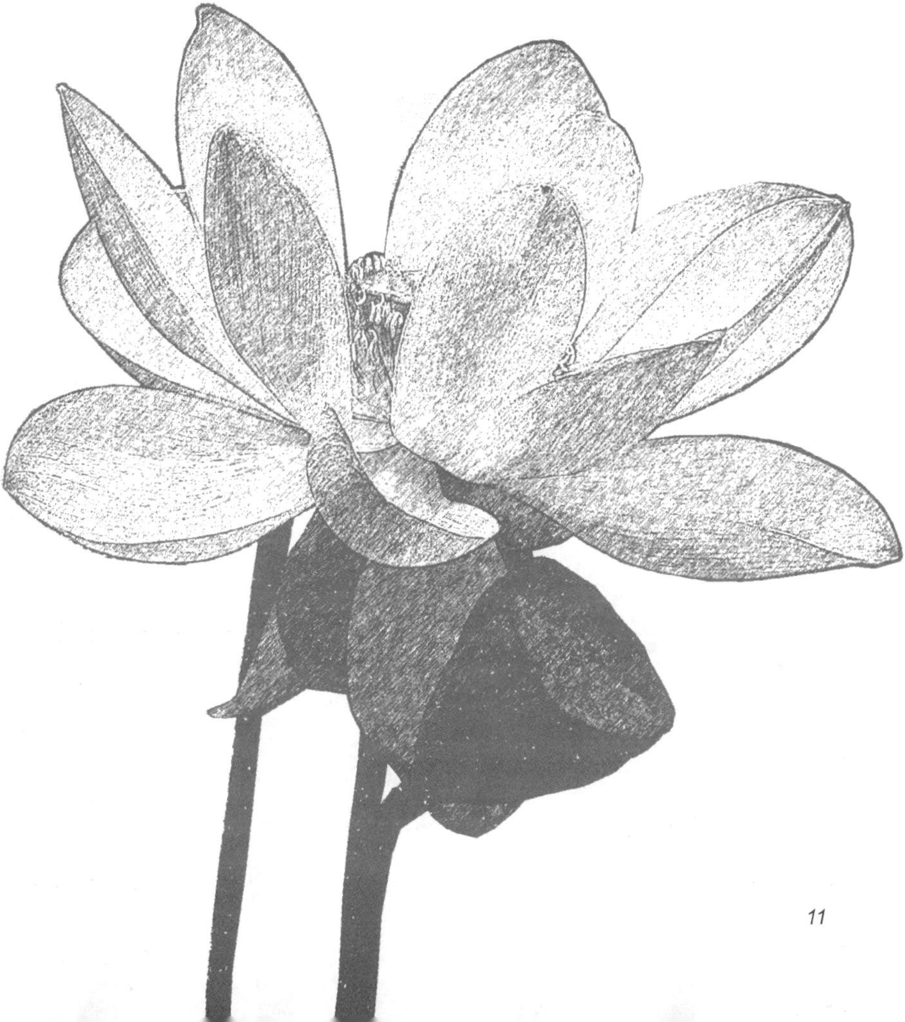

12

Make No Mistake

Even though one of the most inspiring aspects of Buddhism is that one is not expected or even encouraged to 'just believe' in certain teachings or teachers without thoroughly examining them by oneself through wise reflection, investigation and, above all, meditation practice, I believe that it would be an unfortunate mistake to not take the teachings of a great meditation master such as Luang Por Tate seriously and with utmost respect.

In Thailand he is, and was, regarded as one of the truly great beings who succeeded in realizing that exalted peak of human perfection.

Millions of Buddhists know his name. He is revered as an example by so many forest monks who have dedicated their lives to the practice of Dhamma, and even the King of Thailand gave him a title that can hardly be surpassed in the Thai Buddhist culture (Phra Rajanirodharangee).

These translations will provide the reader with the opportunity to hear the Teaching straight from the Heart of a noble master.

Jinavamso Bhikkhu

Sri Lanka 2009

In Pursuit Of The Truth, Learn To Know Nothing

The monk we revere by way of publishing this manuscript––Luang Por Tate—paradoxically "knew" less than any man about everything, but everything about nothing.

As a writer myself, I was delighted that in the midst of my own meditation as to what to write for this introduction, Buddha or someone rather like him, gave me a word, a verb actually—"to unknow."

"Learn to unknow the nonsense you have 'taught' yourself, the home-made assumptions and theories that shackle you, distorting what your heart hears and sees and masking all the joys of the Truth that you might embrace," the Buddha said to me.

"Knowing" so much, the truth is invariably swept aside with a breathtaking arrogance because we think we know so much about the heart, about life and its challenges already. And worse, we think we know better!

This superficial 'knowledge' we admire is entirely unsupported by any proper study or counsel or even real experience, and applying that false knowledge in assessing the need for a spiritual foundation or faith is dangerous indeed. It becomes easy for the young, the not-so-young, and the lazy and the restless to dismiss the need for any commitment in refreshing their spirit, or finding an anchor for the peace of mind they actually deny themselves.

My Buddha says you need to unknow everything before you can truly know anything. And anything is everything in this case—anything is the Buddhist Path to Enlightenment.

Ajahn Sumano Bhikkhu has committed his life to unknowing, and removed himself from the mainstream of frenetic 21st century life in order to have the peace and quiet to empty his mind and to discover the truths that Buddha left for all of us. By not needing to 'know' anything, he moves toward the light of knowing everything—a blessed reality that only he can define.

Suffice to say, layman that I am, ironically his search will require that he embrace the fact that there is nothing there anyway—and that's the beauty of the Buddhist way. In order to understand the smallest fact—that there is nothing there—you must meditate and reflect to the depth of your being and find the calm and peaceful, beautiful and still, warm and welcoming, restful Road-To-Enlightenment.

Finding the Way through meditation is a quest that will repay the dutiful student as he or she unlearns the murky facts that underpin their often directionless modern lives.

To his credit, Ajahn Sumano Bhikkhu never preaches, nor scolds nor harasses those he knows might benefit from following in the Buddha's footsteps. But knowing what he knows already, it almost immediately becomes obvious to those who meet him that we know nothing!

A lifetime of quiet and deep reflection burnishes the spirit, the soul and the heart and there in the place once occupied and wasted by useless knowledge, lives instead the Buddha and the sparkling Path to Enlightenment.

Ajahn Sumano Bhikkhu, quietly contemplating the joys of not knowing in the peaceful forests of Thailand, did not embrace this project because he does not know. If there is but one line of Truth in this book that you stop to underline and use as a mantra to pursue a path that might quiet your heart and give you a sense of rebirth and purpose, then Ajahn Sumano's work will have been well-rewarded.

For it is a giant step for any follower to unknow—or in Buddhist terms to acknowledge their own ignorance, their negligence and their need to purge the harmful "database" of their mind and to re-prioritize in the name of really knowing—that it is time to start over.

Alexander John Pithie

September 2008

Bangkok

Preface

A Reflection For Your Contemplation

Luang Por Tate offers his "Heart" to help all of us in our pursuit.

Like all the forest mendicants, Luang Por Tate's intention is to bring us to the place where we can recognize that our problem is a problem concerning suffering in the body and mind. Obviously, the discomfort of the body is immutable and unsolvable. Whatever position we are in, whether it is sitting, walking, standing or lying down, in no time pain will force us to shift to another posture. However, the suffering in the mind is an add-on and can be solved. The problem has its source in ignorance.

There is a tactic for dealing with the terrorism of ignorance. The cure for suffering in the mind is through mindfulness. Mindfulness is a natural state gravely repressed through modern, conventional education. The thought-proliferation that is encouraged and enhanced through formal education forces the mind to shuttle between back and forth between the past and future. We become oblivious to the present; therefore we cannot see things as they really are. It would be prudent of us to remember the injunction, see things as they are "and the Truth will set you free."

Mindfulness practice, the doorway to the Truth, is designed to re-mind us that wisdom arises only apart from immersion in thought and its proliferation. We also need to know that mental development will never get anywhere if the mind is determined to fixate on things such as a mantra, on a candle, or on inner psychic manifestations. How can wisdom arise or be generated through thinking, through going-with-the-flow, or by contracting the mind? Thinking is always old, it involves memory an unreliable images. Thought is tied to the past. It relies on shifting, unreliable mental images and sensory experience. Making mundane sense out of data spins the mind just as it fuels the 24-hour news channels. Whenever we try to formulate a position or opinion we are pushed into preconceived notions; that is the death of intelligence. How many ideas, opinions, views, and beliefs lock down our lives? Have you ever experienced any improvement in your life through being absolutely "right?" Or even knowing what's "right?"

Real wisdom arises out of the *empty mind* (emboldened with samadhti) which is inclined toward contemplation. *"Empty"* means not holding, not trying, not immersed in mental defilements. And out of that state arises wisdom imbued Insight. What is the point of meditation practice anyway? Only to know the moment as it really is. It's not about changing a thing. We are not getting it right if we are practicing meditation in order to escape, find serenity, or interfere with the changing conditions that temporarily visit the body and mind. That these things began surely necessitates their ending. And in their ending, something new will arise. Everything that arises is destined to leave in its own time… including "you."

Most of us are city people with long, stupefying years shackled into schools and universities and then funneled into offices. All the while engaged in an almost endless cascade of unbroken mental distractions, which I call in-thinking and out-thinking as in "garbage in, garbage out."

How much more on top of your life would you be if you

maintained the awareness that "all things will pass?" What would your life be like if the wanting (and consequent fear) was greatly diminished? Or that you stopped taking things personally?

Some say that becoming Enlightened is an extraordinary feat demanding unrelenting, arduous work. Others say it's easy because we are already Enlightened, we just don't know it. The latter hypothesis asserts that to arrive at "things-as-they-are" is not all that difficult. But, as Luang Por Tate emphasizes, the mind must be trained to attend to the present moment so that awareness of the constancy of change is assured.

The mind must be trained to recognize the conflict constantly plaguing us due to the defilements that contaminate the moment. Additionally, there is the fact that things are happening in several dimensions simultaneously.

On the conventional level, there is a person doing their thing while at the level of ultimate reality there is nothing but a dance of aggregates including bodily form, sensations, perceptions, mental formations, and consciousness, plus the impact of karma, conditioned reactions, hormonal triggers, the wanting-fear syndrome, and a kaleidoscope of emotions moving in and out of center stage in the play of life.

We are swimmers in the surf of change, the quagmire of dissatisfaction, and on the whole, totally unaware of the mind-boggling and implausible fact that there is no one really here. There is no person; never has been one. As for suffering, that predicament can only arise when feelings are misinterpreted as personal. Painful feelings don't demand that we take them as self. We take upon ourselves to own them.

Most of my students have learned to do well in the world. The irony of their success is that they have gotten so stuffed with data, concepts, and opinions that it is now difficult for them to apprehend and to feel the present moment.

Now we come to an essential and crucial point to consider. What is wisdom? It is simply seeing that things are changing, and that something is not quite right—always. And, as I said, that there is no one here. You can't rely on anyone else to bring this home. And you can't look to your instinct or intuition to help you. The Reality is counter-intuitive. What you need to know is not hidden in some book, in some Wat (temple), inside some guru, or buried under an Egyptian pyramid. It's in the present moment. You are bumping into it; you are it, all the time.

What can we do to escape? We can observe the now. If we can watch the body and mind as if it were a robot moving about the idea of self, as we have been trained to believe in, it would disappear. The point is to escape from believing who you think you are and that awareness will extricate you from ever falling under the dominance of suffering.

What is suffering? Why are we so busy trying to flee from it? Is it something that denies pleasure, something that overrides sensual feelings? You will understand more about what the Buddha means by suffering if you recognize that dissatisfaction and conflict is the norm (for 99.999 percent of the people in this world). The quest for happiness is the quest to override the norm. Because it is the norm ("default program"), it's always in the background just waiting for the energy that allowed some temporary happiness to arise, to wear off, and quickly dissipate. When the energy that instigated the pleasure evaporates, unhappiness (suffering) regains its natural place in the order of things.

Finally, some people rely upon retreats to develop their spiritual life. That won't work. If you have a agenda that creates the space for you to retreat for three to four weeks a year you will subconsciously think that it's fine for that "other time" (i.e. "real-world time") to be squandered in unconsciousness. To practice, to come to the end of this tedious, painful saga we must use our everyday life, the stream of present unsatisfactory moments to develop Insight into the-way-things-are.

Ajahn Sumano Bhikkhu

Double-Eyed Cave Sanctuary

June 2009

Keep in Mind

The Buddha Dhamma was one of the Dhammas being taught in India 2,500 years ago. The other "Dhamma" did work. Or, one could say, they worked but didn't cure the problem. What is the problem? Not enough happiness, too much suffering. Unless the factors that start the ball rolling on suffering are quashed, the search for the next dose of happiness will be pursued. All happiness in the world is unsatisfactory.

All the great Ajahns of the northeast of Thailand unanimously point toward awareness in the present moment as the escape hatch. The development of this perspective leads to a sharper, more discriminating mind. And that sharper, more discriminating mind sees through illusion (Maya) and recognizes that all conditions are in the process of change, they are incapable of producing real happiness and there is no actual person in the form that we believe there is. If you can hear what I'm saying you will grasp the Truth of this and see that suffering actually only arises when we believe things are diametrically opposite to reality, imbued with some kind of inherent happiness force and belonging to some permanent entity.

Conditions continuously arise and pass away. Within every condition is the opportunity to see—change, dissatisfaction and non-self ("Tri-luk"; the 3 principles). Everything that arises will always provide access to the "Tri-luk". All suffering arises when the mind is in free float. That mind is busy worrying about the future, regretting the past, wanting some new thing, wanting some old thing to be better-just wanting. But certainly not wanting the end of wanting!

How busy we stay trying to flee from suffering. The point is to escape from believing who you think you, thereby removing the you factor from the power of suffering!

What is suffering? It is not something that denies pleasure or overrides sensual feelings. You will understand what the Buddha means by suffering if you recognize that dissatisfaction and or conflict is the norm. The quest for happiness is the quest to override the norm. Because it is the norm it is always lurking around, always in the background just waiting for the arising energy to wear off. When the energy that instigated the pleasure evaporates, unhappiness (suffering) regains its natural place in the order of things.

The following translated talks are based on the teachings of Ajahn Tate.

Ajahn Luang Por Tate Rangsee
—On "Jit" or Mind

Today I will offer a talk concerning the mind. Actually, the mind is all that I ever I talk about. To talk abut Buddha-Dhamma or the teachings of the Buddha without talking about the mind is impossible. The mind is something much bigger than the entire body. And yet we can't locate the mind.

However, if we don't know the mind we cannot practice. This is the equivalent of looking after a herd of buffalo and cows. We have to fasten the animals to a rope or the animals will just wander off according to their fancy. Once the animals are tied down they won't be confused with options because their range of motion is now limited.

"Boosahngkamang jaykarsarahng ruksakarang poohasarahng yayj ittang poodtameh santi mohk santi ahdtawahnchanah."

This translates as: "The mind has no form; it can wander anywhere."

After the mind has gone off somewhere it returns to the body. If someone can gather the mind together after it has left the body, that person can overcome the problems that result from the body inadvertently doing things in the absence of a mind to control it, in other words, problems that result from carelessness.

The mind of a human being is such that it flits about never staying still.

Don't bother trying to locate the mind because you will never locate this thing called mind. But there is a way you will find the mind. We find the mind through "*knowing*", which occurs when we observe it whenever thought arises, for the mind will arise at the origin of thought. When the mind awakens it is known through feelings and not through the brain or through intelligence transmitted through molecules or cells.

If there were no brain and no cells, the mind would still be there. The mind is known only by way of feeling. Whenever we feel, be it in the feet or on top of the head or anywhere in-between, the mind arises right there, that is where we can know it.

Wherever feeling arises, the mind arises right there. You should train yourself to be aware of exactly where the feeling is arising for there you will find the mind. Having trained yourself you will be able to catch the feeling, catch the thinking. If you catch the thought or the feeling you will have caught the mind. First know the mind then, as the mind thinks, you feel it right in the mind.

When you know the moment as it is, we can call that tying down the mind. This is assures us that our thoughts don't go off in just every direction such as into doubt, the past or future. Keep the awareness right at the place where it arises.

This is how we use awareness (Sati) to control the mind. If you are able to catch the mind at the place where anything arises, proliferation is nipped at the bud. Now you have the mind in its ordinary modality. This is the ordinary mode of mind when it is known right here and now.

When the mind is known (we could say "operating") in this mode, the feelings we are cognizant of will be experienced as neutral.

Knowing the *feeling* will enable you to control the mind. In this balanced and centered manner no thinking runs out. When the thinking is neutralized there is the Heart.

When we speak, regardless of what we are talking about, being in the middle refers to the Heart. The mind is centered and neutralized in the Heart. We have to talk about the mind being centered and neutral, like the physical heart which is located in the middle of the physical body.

The "heart" of one's hand, one's feet or anywhere is in the middle. The Heart doesn't exhibit moral or immoral energies, nor does it veer towards what we call good or bad. This is the state of the real Heart. When there is thinking we must mobilize sati or awareness to follow our thoughts. We utilize sati to catch the mind.

We can follow thought without getting involved in thought. The mind is the tool that thinks linearly and rationally. With sati we can separate and differentiate the mind (jit) from the Heart (jy). That thing which doesn't follow thought- that is the Heart or jy.

When sati knows the thought form as a feeling, the thought will be contained and temporarily be brought to a stop. As soon as the thoughts are caught and stopped, sati transforms them into the Heart.

The reason we have to separate the mind from the Heart is to show that the mind is the thing that thinks, while the

Heart is that which is always empty of thought.

When we utilize sati to capture the mind we will bring the mind and Heart together. When sati purges thought by catching it in time, thought ceases. Then, at that moment, both the mind and Heart come together.

If the mind and heart aren't together we can't say this is metaphysical Heart.

"Eykacharang nisarayang poopasayang": This translates as "The mind is a thing that can wander off into anything and everything."

The body could just be getting ready to act while the mind has run far, far ahead. (In Thai it is said, "Jit pen nai, gy pen bow" or "The mind is the master, the body is the servant.")

As an example, we just sit here and think about going any place in the universe, while our body is just sitting motionless.

We can see that the mind can make the long voyage somewhere and return and make the trip again and again before the body can mobilize itself to make any sort of move. Obviously, we can't bind the mind to force it to wait for the body to make its move. Even if we could control all the doors to the senses, we still couldn't harness the mind.

When the mind moves, it moves on its own. The body has no ability to keep up with the mind. Still, as quick as the mind is, it can never detach from its relationship to the body. When it returns from its forays it returns to the body.

After wandering off, the mind inevitably returns on its own. It returns naturally, for nothing can force it to return. The mind can come together with the Heart and is then beyond the power of the lower realms of hell. This mind cannot be dragged down into hell. In contract, the mind proliferating, the mind floating, is vulnerable to being drawn into the hell realms.

That should be incentive enough for you to bring the mind to merge with the Heart. The mind becomes empty and this emptiness has the power to incline the mind towards Enlightment.

The Buddha separated the hell realm into five categories. Each of these realms has the power to prevent us from either doing good or from attaining freedom, which I shall discuss as follows:

The first realm, called Khandha-**mahn**. This realm concerns our body, which is composed of five components. These are known as the five aggregates. **Rup, Vedena, Sahnyah, Sankhan, and Sunnyah** which necessarily incline towards disintegration through aging and illness.

These five aggregates are obstacles to doing good or progressing in Buddha-Dhamma, the teachings of the Buddha, because they are the catalyst which initiates pain, prevents us from doing our work, and eventually causes death. When they dominate the mind we are unable to generate energy to incline ourselves towards Enlightenment. Or else we are overpowered by laziness, preventing us from doing our duties.

Consider why we call this a "mahn" condition, or in other words, an evil that prevents us from attaining

Enlightenment. You will see that we are born complete with this affliction. Each of these five aggregates works to exploit and distract us.

The second realm or **Kilayt-mahn**. This realm is also an impediment to doing good, both in the present and the future. This impediment involves love, wanting, anger, and stupidity in the mind. These mind states disturb the mind and prevent the mind from attaining tranquility.

For example, when anger has infested the mind, as soon as we bump into someone or something - Wham! Hatred pounces - on something or someone.

These impediments prevent us from progressing in the Buddha-Dhamma. When they are present and active it becomes impossible to practice effectively.

The third realm or **Apisahngkahn-mahn**. This one generates the desire for refined and happy rebirth. Therefore, it is also an obstacle. This hindrance engages us into proliferation in a way, similar to the Devaputtamanh, This hindrance operates in a way that seeks to become more important than others. For instance, one can hope to come back in the next life as a prominent or famous person. This obstacle can shut down our ability even to make offerings, or to be kind.

The fourth realm or **Devaputta-mahn**: This is an obstacle because it draws us into pleasure. This pleasure keeps us stuck in wanting more of the same and, therefore, is a big obstacle because we won't wish to let go and sacrifice this happiness for the possibility of a greater happiness. This obstacle also encourages us to outdo others or to do good with the hidden motivation of getting something extra, something special.

The fifth realm or **Maju-mahn**: This obstacle is the fact of death. Death cuts us off from the opportunity to progress to Nirvana. Death marks the end of our opportunity to do good (or evil, for that matter).

The five impediments or obstacles described above prevent us from gathering the mind together. We are caught in *the world*. While we are still alive and healthy, we should reflect upon the fact that we can develop sati.

This sati together with wisdom will lead toward real Wisdom.

With Wisdom we can take care of our mind so it doesn't wander off, get lost, confused, or fall into doubt, can be brought together and brought into the Heart, as it tends to do. To do this is to escape from these trouble makers. So, right now, we still have the opportunity to get above and beyond the traps laid by the variety of *mahn* or evil agitators.

These conditions keep us trapped in the world and prevent us from reaching the Path. Most people look at *mahn* - the various evils - as frightening and surrender to them; in a sense, surrendering to our baser instincts. The Buddha taught us not to surrender. The Buddha said the *mahn* were the most important things to work with.

Like the Buddha himself, through meditation we can cleanse ourselves of the *mahn*. The Buddha became the Enlightened One by outwitting the *mahn*. "Gumjutmalay soonee naso munboso muttamahng".

You might think that since the body of the Buddh? same before and after he attained Enlightment, nou. really changed! In fact, what changed was inside.

The Buddha no longer got caught by any of the varieties of *mahn*. Having established the causes, Enlightenment evolved on its own. For us too, it is critical that we disengage from the *mahn*. The Buddha said that one could triumph against the *mahn* by not clinging to the misunderstanding that the body is our personal thing.

The Buddha reached Enlightenment by letting go of the idea of a personal body and mind through seeing that there is just this arising and just this passing away. To overcome the *mahn* the Buddha used the principle that everything should be contemplated through the lenses of Annicam, Dukkhum, and Annata. (uncertainty, suffering, and none-self).

Life, when viewed through the three lenses, will enable us to overpower the mahn. This practice took the Buddha beyond the dominance of the mahn.

The Buddha then taught us how to apply the same principles to overcome the *mahn*. We should contemplate and reflect that everything involved with the body is composed of only the five aggregates or, from another point of view, four elements (earth, air, fire, and water).

Everything that arises is the result of karma or action. Don't continue to look at the body as being composed of legs, arms, head and feet. It is, rather, solely composed of the four elements of earth, air, fire, and water in a variety of physical combinations. These things arise and pass away. Why would we want to grasp onto anything that arises and passes away? It's all *annata* (non-self). That being the reality, there is no sense to grasp on to any such transient aspects.

Each of the four elements is the main constituent in the various organ systems of the body (i.e. blood-water). These four elements arise and pass away. There are not any "persons" as such. People are just combinations of the elements. They arise and pass away. Why would you want to grasp onto things that arise and pass away (and which you have no ability to control)?

In reality we are unable to grasp onto them because they are continuously in the process of change. This is called the principle of *annata*—or annicam. Annicam, Dukkham and Annata (uncertainty, suffering, and non-self) are intrinsically connected.

You can focus on any single one of these principles and you will be able to see them all. When you do, you will see the truth of things-as-they-are. The first two principles, annicam and dukkham, were known before the time of the Buddha.

But until the time of the Buddha, no one could see the principle of Annata for it is a very demanding and challenging thing to see. This factor <u>always</u> exposes itself but it is very hard to distinguish.

If you can't quite do this you need to first calm the mind and allow it to settle down. Gathering the mind is something each of us has to do for ourselves. This is something that can be done only if you relinquish your compulsive concern with matters of the world, and if you are determined to live in a way that doesn't cause troubles or problems for others. Gathering and composing the mind is a personal matter. Everyone is capable of doing it. Not only will you achieve a peaceful state of mind, you will also stop creating misery for others.

Your efforts will benefit yourself and your country. If everyone made their mind peaceful this entire world would be peaceful. By doing so, no one's minds would be thinking of ways to harm others. In a group of 100 or 1,000 people if there is just one person who can gather his/her mind together, that one person will certainly positively and profoundly affect the whole group in a positive manner.

Nowhere did the Buddha teach that a whole group of people would suddenly and spontaneously observe and contemplate their minds, but rather everything could improve through the development of one courageous individual at a time.

On the other hand, if everyone's mind is inclined toward harming others, it is certain that there will be endless conflict. Therefore, gathering your mind, taking care of your mind is a critically important responsibility that we have to ourselves and others, if we assume that we are to live in peace and harmony with others.

When your mind is calm and peaceful no one will be able to disturb or irritate you. Whatever problems you are having in your life, these problems won't have the power to disturb or overwhelm you. This principle is similarly true concerning the world at large. No matter how chaotic things are in the world, that chaos won't agitate someone who is calm and at peace.

Remember well this principle---No matter how crazy the

world becomes, if you meditate and learn to settle your mind the problems of the world won't agonize or distress you. If the world gets to the point that it is on the verge of breaking apart, that still won't disturb the peaceful mind. You won't go running out into the chaos. Rather, you will turn your attention to your Heart.

There is a story that in one of the Buddha's earlier lives, the Buddha-to-be was a wandering sage (though still not of the caliber of a Buddha). At that time the wife of a spirit-dragon, having heard the teaching of the sage, asked her husband to fetch the heart of the wise man for her admiration. ****

The spirit-dragon thought she wanted the physical heart of the wise man so he set out to find and kill the sage and take his heart. Actually when she said *heart* she was referring to the refined and deep spiritual teachings of the mendicant. She wanted the essence or Heart of his wisdom transmitted to her, not literally his physical heart.

When the spirit-dragon met the wise man on the road, the sage knew immediately the mind of the spirit-dragon. He tried to shift his perspective by offering him a noble Teaching but the spirit-dragon couldn't hear what was being said as he was preoccupied with his plot.

So the sage spoke a second time, but again the heavy karma of the spirit-dragon was too much of a barrier for him to actually hear and be cognizant of the teachings. The sage understood that this was his karma. There might not be a way to avoid his fate.

Still, the wise man decided to offer one last short

teaching, in which he made it clear to the spirit-dragon that regardless of what the spirit-dragon intended to do to him, he would maintain his unshakeable, calm and happy demeanor and bearing.

"Manoot tung lai pen poo beeat beean sueng gun la gun. Row yoo pen sook nor. Manoot tung lai pen wayn seunggun la gun. Row yoo pen sook dee."

The rough translation is: "All wise beings necessarily come to know this Truth. Regardless of what people do in their lives, this Truth is eternal."

The sage's statement moved the spirit-dragon. He understood the essence and implications of this teaching and he immediately let go of his fiendish resolve. Then, he politely guided the sage back to his home for the benefit of his wife. What he had delivered to her was the sage's Heart, the best and highest teachings she had ever heard.

This story illustrates how people who gather their minds and thereby acquire wisdom can go anywhere, face any dangers and will always be safe.

Another important point for us to contemplate in this story is that when the spirit-dragon went out looking for the wise man, his intention was not selfish. We shouldn't overlook that. He searched for the sage in order to carry out his wife's request. In his mind, even though he was setting out to kill someone, he thought he was doing a good thing.

However, since he was under the influence of his heavy and dark karma which activated various defilements, these dark energies set him off on an unskillful course of action.

His mind was agitated and completely under the influence of his karma, so he wasn't able to see the right course of action that was appropriate in the situation. We can see that since the sage had long stilled his mind he could act with discernment and awareness.

This illustrates how making the mind peaceful is the single most important thing people can do for themselves. When one is agitated in this way it is the result of the mind thinking, thinking, thinking. When we make the mind relinquish this meaningless proliferation (the same factors that make the mind peaceful are present here), that thinking mind turns in and gathers into the Heart.

The mindfull-less actions occurring in the mind are the business of the mind. When you are mindful and bring it into the Heart, you transform it into something worthwhile for yourself. If you practice in this manner, you will be following the Path of the Buddha.

Through your practice you will be able to gather everything into the heart and will no longer be bothered by anything at all. The visa for entering into Nirvana is settling the mind into peace and, thus, transforming the mind into the Heart.

This brings me to the end of my talk for today.

The Rice Plant

In today's talk I will be comparing the Buddha's meditation practice with a rice plant. We need to have something to compare the Buddha's Teaching with in that the teachings are rather refined. I will compare the Buddha's Teaching with something that we already know. Otherwise we won't be able to identify the characteristics properly.

To begin with, let us understand that all of us are born with certain defilements, in the form of desires, wants and cravings, that are an integral part of our lives and which must be cleansed and extinguished. For the defilements to be cleansed and extinguished effectively, they must be dealt with in particular and specific ways. Why we should endeavor to cleanse and extinguish our defilements will become apparent.

In approaching the challenge of cleansing and extinguishing our defilements, we can compare ourselves to a tree. Easier still, we can compare ourselves with a rice plant. We can use a grain of rice to highlight the comparison.

Each rice plant grows from just one seed. We take this one seed and plant it into the wet earth. One seed, one plant. If the earth is fertile the seed of the rice will develop beautifully and will produce the maximum number of seeds.

From these seeds many more plants can be bred. Where does the original seed come from? I don't know. How does the plant develop? I don't know.

To begin with there was no roots, no stem, no leaf and then-there they are! What I do know is that because there is both water and earth the seed will burst open and mature. It will establish itself and become a fully grown rice plant. We know that if the earth is fertile, the plant will generate many more plants from this one seed. Over time, the seed becomes fully mature producing many benefits. Each grain of rice contains the whole plant. The important point for us to recognize here is that the kernel of the rice seed is inherent within the seed.

Compare this with ourselves. Our defilements operate quite differently. Let's look at ourselves. When we are born we are born as helpless infants. We don't have many variations as to how we conduct ourselves. When we outgrow childhood, we enter the teenage period. Following that period we become adults. We can call ourselves adults once we arrive at the point where we understand our society and our culture adequately. We may then marry and start our own family.

Unbeknownst to us the defilements within us are growing along with our life. This can be seen when we begin to spawn desires to have this and that and to be someone special. We foster the desire to be praised and recognized as someone important. As we become older our desires expand and multiply. In addition to wanting more for ourselves, we want more for our family and friends.

But that's not the end of it. Wanting doesn't just stop at one's family and friends but reaches further and further out. There is craving for more and more, even without knowing why we want more and more. In fact, there is no point of saturating this desire to get more and more for ourselves or others. There is always the feeling of *still not enough* lurking about, and continuing all the way up until the day we die. This hunger, this wanting-this and wanting-that, is insatiable and never comes to an end.

We never feel that we ever have enough even though our lives revolve around trying to satisfy our various wants. We are constantly reaching out to acquire more and more, more of this and more of that, forever wanting, even on our own death bed. The Buddha said that this wanting-wanting syndrome is so voracious that it inundates and overflows the world. Actually, he taught, not just this world which we know but this feeling of deficiency spills over right into the next world as well.

Note this situation is quite unlike what we see in a rice grain. When the seed is ripe the entire future of the plant-to-be is contained in the seed. The farmer is content, for he knows that these rice grains will be ideal for planting the next season's crop. The rice seedling is a perfect example of how everything can congregate into one place.

In contrast, a human being full of defilements isn't able to bring together all his or her negative factors into one place. In our practice of cleansing and extinguishing our defilements we should strive to have the mind pull together all these factors in the same way as we see it done in a grain of rice. But what we do, on the contrary, is attach to the defilements in a way that assures they will get involved, to a greater and greater extent, with the ear, eye, nose, tongue, body feelings and mind.

The reality is that there are many varieties of defilements exhibiting them selves by way of the sense doors. For example, when there is a desire arising from what we see with our eyes, we fixate on that attractive form and seek to acquire it for ourselves. The defilement takes hold inducing a train of thoughts, desires, and associated proliferation. If we compare this process to a rice plant it would be the same as if, after planting the rice seed, that seed expanded out beyond its husk, expanding further and further and further over time. The net result would the same as when a single rice seed reproduces itself through many, many generations.

But in the case of the defilements, time is not much of a factor as desire expands farther and farther out. For instance, when the eye sees a form it likes, defilement arises. Once liking/disliking, loving/hating arises and we grasp onto it through identification, we set in motion a train of thought-forms. The defilements keep expanding, compounding and multiplying through contact with phenomena as they are experienced at the sense doors. What we experience at the sense doors are forms, tastes, smells, sounds, body feelings, and mental constructions. When defilements are mixed with these factors, greed, anger and ignorance are sure to arise. Every single germ of adulteration encompasses greed, anger and ignorance.

As an example, consider love. Notice that hate arises from love. All manner of danger arises from love. Sorrow arises from love. All this vulnerability follows from the initial action of clinging. However, if we observe love and all the other defilements through the lens of *Dhamma*, or the Teachings of the Buddha, we will see that they arise from within our mind. We also see that our relationship to our mind is the source and cause of our trouble.

We can halt the process right in its tracks, if we can catch these defilements in the mind before they arise. We must catch them through the application of the *Dhamma*, the Teachings of the Buddha. By applying *Dhamma* we can discover that these negative energies can go through the mind, gather together into the Heart, then pass out safely as *Buddha-Dhamma*. When we catch phenomena as they arise, they can gather in the Heart as one thing just as in the rice seed, where the roots, the stem and the leaf all come together.

The defilements arise out of the mind. The mind, not the Heart, is the source of all defilements. If we are going to catch the defilements we have to catch them where they arise, in the mind. The way to catch the defilements is through mindfulness-*sati* (in other words, an awareness of the machinations of the mind). When we employ mindfulness-*sati* the defilements come together in the mind under the authority of *sati*, rather than set off to agitate the mind causing all sorts of trouble for us.

Sati or the necessary pre-wisdom factor gathers everything together into the Heart. This is like the rice seed which incorporates all the aspects of the rice plant before being planted. We can't see the defilements and destroy them until they first arise and exhibit themselves. As soon as the defilements arise we can catch them and neutralize them by using wisdom- *punnyah*. Wisdom is the factor in our consciousness which can see and catch every sort of defilement. Awareness is the factor that catches the defilements while wisdom is the factor that extinguishes it. Those dedicated and heroic meditators who can extinguish all defilements, from coarse to refined, we call *Ariya*. We shouldn't be anxiety-ridden about the defilements continuously intruding on our consciousness, for it's only after they arise that we have the opportunity to eradicate them.

We don't have to be a detective and search here and there when we go after the defilements in order to clean them out. All defilements including love, hate, anger, jealousy, all convene right here in the mind. Here we can clean out the defilements totally until what remains is the pure mind. We can call it extinguishing, letting go and throwing away, brushing away or pulling out. It all comes to the same thing and accomplishes the same end. However, most people don't have the wisdom to do it. They allow the defilements to affix onto the mind. Once the defilements take hold they expand in influence and power. Therefore it's important to firmly establish *sati* which will assure that defilements don't grow and become more and more powerful.

These defilements are the casual factor that forces rebirth. Through practice, we have to rid ourselves of the defilements until we get to the point where we are so fed up with the syndrome of liking and not liking, loving and hating that we are no longer disturbed or affected by them. The mind returns to the center. When more defilements arise it is because there are many levels of negative, dark energies...some deeper and more devious than we imagine. Then, if a person is truly intent on release, he/she must maintain their meditative intention in order to subjugate the innumerable defilements as they arise, regardless of the form or variation and regardless of how subtle or refined their manifestation. Love and hate may arise, delight and aversion may arise. All manner of defilements may arise. It is the job of the meditator to bring up maximum energy to deal with them. We deal with them without bias and without hope.

Keep in mind that if you find that you can only catch one mind-moment of defilement and you are able to deal with it effectively, you can justly feel satisfied. In doing so you have achieved the thing that is of the most benefit to a human being, and indicates that you are capable of completing this work. Also, keep in mind, that this is not your first life time. You have been born and reborn countless times. During that measureless period of time you have been storing up defilement energy. Defilement and *karma* (or intentional actions) can be regarded as one and the same thing, because even though some of your *karma* is positive, most of it is negative.

A person who has trained and developed acute wisdom can catch and clear out the defilements as soon as they arise. In contrast, someone with less wisdom can only see and catch the defilements after they have made themselves obvious. Still, regardless of how much wisdom people may have, they can employ whatever they have to cleanse the defilements. They can accomplish the same end. In other words, both the person with a lot of wisdom and the person with a bit of wisdom are capable of extinguishing the defilements.

If you cannot be bothered to cut out the defilements you can be sure that they will expand and grow. If you attempt to pull out a plant but don't extract the entire root system, that which is still in the ground will become *even stronger* as soon as the factors are right, coming back one hundred times, one thousand times more vigorously than was the case in the beginning.

Because of this fact we have to depend upon *sati* or mindfulness-awareness to look after the mind at all times and in all postures. If we are negligent concerning the mind, the defilements will spread out like rice seeds going out in every direction, or like the spores of a plant blowing and fanning out over a large area.

Therefore we must have *sati* to oversee the mind completely. This factor will prevent the defilements from roaming freely and constantly causing trouble. We must recognize the need to clean out the defilements right at the source so there is nothing whatsoever left. If we don't do a thorough job of completely cleaning out the defilements at the source, the power of the defilements will be the causal fact that sustains the cycle of being born, dying, being born, dying, being born, dying, etc., etc., together with all the suffering we have to go through over the course of each and every lifespan.

If we are oblivious to the situation there will be no end to our predicament. However, there will come a time when we can discern the problem involved with suffering. Once that insight arises, existential boredom follows. When we see this existential boredom and how it relates to the very fact of rebirth, the mind releases its tendency to embrace the pursuit of pleasure and the hunger for the flavor of the things that previously seemed pleasurable. The mind drops its pursuit of all the things belonging to the world. This is an integral process involved in *cleansing the mind*. Thereupon the mind refuses to cling to pleasure, to love, etc. The mind is now balanced and neutral (*upaka*).

Because the variations of the defilements are stacked up within many levels, if and when they arise again we must clean them out in the same manner. Our job as meditators is to vigorously and continuously clean them out (*viraya}*. To do this we have to employ mindfulness/*sati*. We have to be careful not to be fooled, for sometimes we may think we have an acute understanding of things as-they-are but in reality the truth is deeper and more refined than we recognize.

The end of the Path requires more of us than we can envision. In order to see clearly we need to cleanse the defilements continuously. If, using *sati*, we endeavor to continuously clear out the defilements, we will have done something of tremendous benefit for ourselves. If we manage to cleanse ourselves of defilements even just one time, what arises in that moment is a sense of satisfaction which suggests "that's it", *finis*. We could be misled into thinking that there are no defilements left…we are utterly pure! However, when the mind makes contact with situations that bring up love or hate, the mind goes on to wildly proliferate. When we are happy with something or unhappy with something we become biased either positively or negatively. That being the case we have obviously duped ourselves into thinking that we are pure.

We will see that in certain situations, these hidden positive-negative energy forces will arise on their own because they are still a potent force within us. Anyone determined to progress in practice can expect to run into this mistaken assessment. We must understand that since we have been born and reborn more times than we can imagine or count, throughout that period of time the defilements have been accumulating. Throughout this long period of life-cycles the defilements have grown stronger and stronger.

Actually, both doing unskillful actions *and* doing skillful or good actions involve the defilements, involve *karma*. Both possibilities arise out of *karma*. For *karma* and defilements are intertwined. The fact is that we have been doing mostly foolish, unskillful things over the course of countless lifetimes. We have behaved wisely far less often. Just watch what's going on over the course of one day and you will see how many more unskillful mind-moments arise as opposed to skillful ones! For the most part you don't yet have the ability to see the defilements before they arise. The defilements have more power than your power to neutralize them. That's the way it is, even for those of you who have practiced long and hard. You don't have the mental power to see the defilements in time. Many years can go by without seeing your situation. This is the way it is because the defilements are stronger than our ability to see, the power of our *samadhti*.

When you cleanse defilements you experience a kind of happiness. Therefore we must be determined and keep forging ahead. This is our situation, not someone else's. We must do it ourselves if we want to rectify the problem. For someone just starting out and recognizing the difficulty in bringing the mind together, know that if over the course of a year or two you are able to develop some *samadhti* and get on top of the defilements, that is no small achievement. Don't get discouraged when progress is slow and difficult.

When the mind has come together you have reached the stage where you are beginning to cleanse the mind. From then on your progress will be the force that reduces the power of the defilements. If you don't have concentration underpinning the mind, your mind will continue indefinitely with its habit of clutching onto the defilements. Doing this work is not something easy. But, it's also not something beyond our ability. Anyone who puts themselves into this work will, I assure you, one day become Enlightened. The Buddha taught but one practice, only the way to make your mind pure. Every aspect of his teachings points to this end result. If this Path didn't lead to escape, the Buddha wouldn't have taught it.

Cleansing yourself of all your defilements will take time. If over the course of all your lifetimes you did nothing but unskillful, foolish deeds, there is no chance that you could ever become Enlightened. What would you have to grow from? That is not your case. If you are seeking to become free, you have to reduce the power of the defilements and, finally, eradicate them. In the meantime, we must avoid storing up more defilements.

This is the same as the principle which applies to the principle operating in the conventional world. If we want something badly we have to accumulate that thing. We must increase our assets. Or, from the perspective of Dhamma, we must refrain from accumulating impediments to that which we desire. For instance, whenever we make offerings to monks, we feel happy. This is because on that occasion of giving, the defilements are not able to arise. We seek happiness so we act in a way which brings us happiness. The more we understand how this works the more we are inclined to develop charity and generosity.

Making offerings is a refined and elegant gesture which cuts away greed, hatred and ignorance. When we express generosity we feel a wave of delight. At this point in our life we still have plenty of coarse defilements. However, if we understand the Law of Karma and how the results of our actions affect our lives, we will determine to maintain either the 5, 8, 10, or 227 precepts (do good, don't do evil) as an intelligent way to control ourselves and as the *way* to cleanse and, eventually, purify the defilements.

In the beginning, we might maintain just one or two precepts. Then, we might feel ready to take on the others until we are maintaining all five or eight precepts. When we maintain the precepts, this acts as a brake against unskillful behavior and cleanses our mind. But don't think this is an easy thing to do. In any case, this isn't meant to imply that merely maintaining the precepts will take you all the way to Enlightement. This is the most skillful way to avoid doing evil while at the same time inclining towards doing good. Living under these precepts allows us to add more goodness and less evil to our karmic stream.

When we practice *Samadhti* the mind will be cool and peaceful as it comes to a state of contentment. This mind will automatically let go of any sort of evil. When we are able to do this, we extricate ourselves from the malignant power of the defilements. Slowly but surely we sanitize ourselves from the defilements using wisdom to eradicate them. The functioning of wisdom is the critical aspect of mentality that can guard and inform us about the danger involved with unskillful actions and to direct us away from foolish behavior. Clearly, wisdom arises from first maintaining the precepts.

With the precepts as a refuge, *samadhti* can develop. With *samadhti*, the mind will cool and calm down and come to peace. And we will be able to contemplate the means for eradicating the defilements. Through our practice the defilements will slowly lose power and eventually disappear. What is left is simply the pure mind. This is the way to cleanse ourselves of the defilements. The more we generate *Samadhti* the more energy we bring to the development of wisdom which will eventually enable us to progress in *vipassana* (i.e., move towards seeing the Truth of life, not the ordinary cleverness we see in the everyday world). This wisdom is the kind that knows everything the mind is up to and sees everything in terms of *annican, dukkham, annata*.

At the peak level of wisdom, we will see that everything that arises is in a state of flux, is at least somewhat unsatisfactory, and is not-self. We arrive at the end point where we see with confidence that EVERYTHING is under the authority of these three factors. This insight comes from the result of our single-minded awareness, where *vipassana* initiates wisdom. This is called cleansing the mind. This is the Path. But this is not the end of the story. Wisdom arises from underlying conditions. No one can make it arise otherwise.

This is what makes wisdom so amazing. It arises on it own and establishes itself on its own. You are now on the track, taking you to the point where you must make use of *Vipassana* to come to *Nirvana*. We must contemplate *annica, dukkkham and annata*. If you want to come to the end of the work you have to come to this *real-ization.*

The wisdom that arises out of *vipassana* practice is the wisdom that cannot be brought forth through thought, but can only arise from practice. Indeed, the *Dhamma* of the Buddha is a remarkable thing which only arises when you see for yourself, through the step-by-step development of your practice.

So here I have elucidated the six steps necessary for developing the mind. To summarize they are generosity, morality, the development of concentration, the development of wisdom, enhanced concentration, and finally, wisdom at the heart of *vipassana*.

The Path of Practice—(Nayo Patibut)

Because the Buddha's Teaching is rather refined, we need to have something to compare the Buddha's Teaching with. We need to compare the Buddha's Teaching with something we already know or are familiar with, otherwise we won't be able to identify the characteristics properly. To begin with, let us understand that all of us are born with certain defilements, in the form of desires, wants and cravings, that are an integral part of our lives and which must be cleansed and extinguished. For the defilements to be cleansed and extinguished effectively, they must be dealt with in particular and specific ways. Why? That we should endeavor to cleanse and extinguish our defilements will become apparent later on.

Thus, today I will offer a talk on how Buddhism is practiced using the analogy of a tree. I am offering this talk in order to provide practitioners, both Buddhist and non-Buddhist, with the knowledge to enable them to practice properly for their benefit, because the practice of Buddhism through meditation is in fact independent of whether or not one believes in Buddhism.

Although the practice of meditation can be discussed independently of Buddhism, I shall discuss it in its Buddhist context, insofar as meditation is an integral part of Buddhism. The Buddhist religion has been around for more than 2500 years, but over the centuries the religion has passed through some dark ages. In this regard, I am referring to the people who profess to be Buddhists rather than the religion itself. Regardless of the state of things, there will always be the Buddha and the Path of Practice, along with other skills that the Buddha taught us.

During the dark ages, people had more difficulty understanding the teachings and the skillful instructions of the Buddha. The fact is that the Buddha's teachings are both profound and refined. To understand his teachings requires a light mind. People who endeavored to practice during those times had considerable difficulty in understanding and practicing what the Buddha taught. They did not have enough *light* to work with.

Actually, even in the best of times, if people listen to Dhamma-Desana, i.e., Teachings of the Buddha on a daily basis, they still have their everyday work to attend to and that is quite a hurdle for them for them to get over. When their minds are focused and centered while listening to a Dhamma-Desana, that mindfulness will allow them to increase their understanding of Dhamma, or the Teachings of the Buddha. However, when they return to their everyday duties, they tend to forget what they have learned. The nature of their lives makes it difficult for them to retain and integrate the understanding that recently came to them.

I will offer you an overview of the practical side of Buddhism, especially for those of you who have many duties in the world. Actually every time I give a talk on Buddhism, I talk only and directly about the Path of practice. Even though I always talk in terms of the Buddhist religion in which the practice of meditation is grounded, I would like to emphasize again that the practice of Buddhism, as manifested in meditation, is in fact independent of the religious precepts, and can therefore be practiced by people of any religious denomination. Now, I will integrate the various ways I talked about the Path of Practice taught by the Buddha, so that you can understand his principles easily.

We can talk about the Buddha's Teachings as the means for providing all the things that you could wish for- the things that everyone desires.

To make it easy for all of you to understand the Buddha's Teachings, I will use a tree to compare the structure of the Buddha Dhamma.

Just like a tree, the Buddhist religion has bark, cambium, and core. These components, working together, have enabled Buddhism to carry on for a relatively long time. If there was only a core, Buddhism would not have been able to sustain itself for long. The religion would not be able to endure. No tree can live for long with only a core. Each layer of the tree protects and serves the deeper internal layers. A tree requires both the outer and inner layers so that it can grow through the various stages of its development and reach full maturity. Just as the outer layers depend on the core, the core depends on all the outer layers for support and nourishment.

Right up until today the Teachings of the Buddha have remained more or less intact. In terms of the Buddha's Teachings, what exactly do the layers of bark, cambium, and core mean?

The outer-most layer is the least significant layer. At the "bark level" there are the rituals we see which are connected and affiliated with the religion, such as invitations for monks to deliver sermons or talk about Buddhist precepts, the invitation for monks to offer auspicious chanting, as well as other invitations. These are peripheral matters. So what are they for? They are there to elicit inner resolve and fortitude (for these energies are the beginning point in practice). The energy of commitment is necessary so that one can keep the precepts and listen to talks on the Dhamma. The bark is also the layer that encourages accumulation of "boon", or merit, through generosity, or the act of giving (*tumboon*).

GENEROSITY, OR THE ACT OF GIVING, PROVIDES THE OPPORTUNITY TO MAKE MERIT BY OFFERING THINGS TO MONKS, NOVICES AND NUNS.

The things that are offered make it possible for the ordained community to survive because, according to their rules, monks and novices are not allowed to work in agriculture or hold down any jobs i.e. work for remuneration. They dedicate themselves solely to deepening their understanding of the Buddha's Dhamma or teachings. Also, at this layer there are the special ceremonies at which monks chant using a special melodic chanting mode while recounting the previous lives of the Buddha. One can listen deeply and reflect on how Prince Gautama developed the qualities that resulted in his becoming the Buddha or "Enlightened One".

Continuing with the tree analogy, we come to the next layer which is the cambium. This layer covers the necessary foundation of morality...the 5th, 8th, 10th, and 227th precepts of Buddhism. If one's precepts are in place one can gain access to the core of the religion. Buddhists who make offerings of things and gifts only, but don't bother to maintain the moral precepts, prevent themselves from entering to the core of Buddhism. The offerings of people who don't keep the precepts are not always pure. Some of the things they offer could have been acquired by way of lying, killing animals, corruption, stealing, drugs or deception. That which is gained through destructive or harmful behavior won't spiritually benefit anyone. This is the cambium. This layer is important as it requires keeping the precepts, essentially the five restraints on behavior, (killing sentient beings, deceiving, improper sexuality, speaking falsely and coarsely and using intoxicants. The 5, 8, 10, and 227 precepts are concerned entirely with how to behave ethically, i.e., what to do to refrain from harmful or destructive behavior. When we learn how to behave ethically, we can access the core of the religion. Once we go beyond the cambium, we are at the starting point for the genuine practice of Buddhism by way of meditation, because we have worked though the outer levels and are now in a position to really progress in meditation.

When doing so, we will not engage in behavior inappropriate for human beings. Our actions will be clear and clean. We will be utterly confident in the power of the Triple Gems (Buddha, Dhamma, and Sangha) and be absolutely resolute in our innate wisdom based on the belief in the Buddha's Teachings. When we reach the Core, we can practice in order to instruct the mind to maintain the precepts in order not to have chaos or turbulence in our lives.

The mind can settle into samadhti (the state of being

focused) so that there is development in practice (the energy factor). When the mind is clear and pure, we say that we have reached the Core. The highest and best use of a tree is when everything comes together in the Core.

The bark and the cambium are now ready to be of real benefit to us. While we can make use of these outer layers, their value alone is limited. That which is of most benefit is the Core. The core of a tree is useful for building a house, for use as a post for building a house and the like. We use the core for construction, not the bark or the cambium. But the bark and epidermis are critical for protecting the core so that we can make good use of the nucleus in building a house. If tree doesn't have core, most people probably wouldn't want it. Trees such as banana trees or papaya trees, which mature without a core, are not robust. This is true, as well, for trees that have a very short life span. Whereas hardwood trees that grow slowly, 100 years to 1000 years before reaching the end of their lifespan, all have cores. People who reach the Core of Buddhism are defended and protected in the best possible way. When they meet suffering of any kind, they find that their hearts are strong and unwavering. Like strong trees, they don't get knocked over in a storm.

The Buddha saw that once human beings are born, they are immediately trapped in a swamp of suffering. Most people aren't able to see the enormity of their suffering. This is because they can't see things clearly, as they are. They never really look at the situation in which suffering is embedded. Why? Because they are always distracted by things that they hope will make them feel happy, excited, or delighted.

Some people refuse to look at the fact of suffering because they feel it will make them anxious and depressed. They believe that they are somehow born into this life, that this is all there is, so they might as well just use it to get as much pleasure as they can. Some people who suffer a lot and cannot find a way out of their suffering choose to solve the problem by getting and staying drunk or using intoxicants. The strange idea they are caught up in is that they think that they can forget their problems through intoxication.

The virus that initiates suffering is there right from the time we are in the womb, right through to the moment we die. Through our whole life cycle we encounter all varieties, all magnitudes, and all forms of suffering. Don't forget that there is suffering even before we leave the womb.

Then, there is anguish in trying to find a livelihood. Finding work, we make money. However, if we don't spend it, of what consequence is the money? So we spend it, and once spent, we have to work to get more.

The money we make that is in excess of our needs is of no real value for us. However, there is a limitless supply of things that money can buy, and we automatically expand our "needs" in step with any money we acquire. Suffering (dukkha) sets in when we have insufficient funds to fulfill our so-called "needs".

Both the poor and rich have to deal with this situation. Therefore the business of making money throws us into this squirrel cage of suffering.

Clearly, the problem of making a living is complicated. To say it bluntly, the problem of having "enough" to eat, a place to sleep, etc. is an impossible one to resolve when *enough-ness* is an ever-expanding and unattainable goal. This is true for everyone, except for someone who is born into this world who is able to delimit the boundaries of *enough-ness*!

Suppose we were to live our life as a frog. Most of the time the frog has to eat normally, however, there are times in the year when the frog hibernates for a long period in his burrow. He encloses himself in a tiny chamber leaving just a small opening for an air duct. During those times there is little rain and the water holes tend to dry up. These are the times when there is nothing for the frog to eat. When the frog goes into hibernation, while he eats nothing, nonetheless the frog has to urinate and eliminate solid waste. For some reason this causes the frog to become softer and fatter. At this time the frog is tastier than when he is out jumping around hunting for food. The obvious significance here is that the life of a frog is somewhat easier than the life of a person. Frogs don't have to pursue the business of eating continually and with no end in sight. When they hibernate, they only have to be concerned with urinating and eliminating solid waste. However after the hibernation period (two or three months) the frog has to go out and find food again. The frog must again face the suffering involved in maintaining itself in the world. All humans born into this world have at least some degree of suffering when it comes to obtaining the requisites necessary to sustain themselves.

The situation for monks and novices is a bit different. They are not permitted to go out and sell things in the market, engage in agriculture, nor pursue a layman's livelihood. If they want to eat they must go out on their morning alms round and accept offerings of food. To a large extent they go out for offerings because it is their duty to provide the opportunity for lay people to make merit while spreading loving kindness into the world. The offerings that lay people put into their bowls are the things necessary to sustain the life of a Buddhist monk or "samana".

Even after the Buddha attained enlightenment, he still needed to go out for alms and to eat like everyone else. Having to obtain food and having to eat involves suffering. Although everyone has to do it, it is not the same for everyone. It all depends on the mind and heart of each individual. For most people, who aren't interested in the Buddha-Dhamma or the Teachings of the Buddha, when they are having a meal, they resent having to pay for it.

They display the characteristics of a stingy person. Deep inside they feel that they have to work hard to make a living and should, somehow, be entitled to eat without spending much. The fact is, if you only eat a little bit, you won't have to pay very much for what you eat. If you eat a lot, you should pay a lot for it. It is appropriate to pay for what one gets. That is fair. That is just. People who think they should be entitled to eat but not pay their fair share need to overcome their stinginess.

For example, there are sometimes leftovers when we eat. One should store leftovers for the times when there isn't enough. Also, you can make use of these stored surpluses when you need food for your children and grandchildren. Don't be stingy! Reflect on the fact that no one can take anything along with them when they die.

Look at this surplus as ordinary, not as something too special to touch. The things we struggle so hard to get can't go along with us when we die. All our "stuff" is inherited by the universe. Actually, as for the things we accumulate, the most sensible and judicious way to make use of these things comes not from the holding and guarding but from the act of giving away. For through our generosity we receive the *boon* or merit from our offering and that alone is something that does go with us after death, according to Buddhist belief.

There are many skillful ways to make use of our things. We can offer our things to poor people, or to relatives in need. Or we can give these things to our parents to assure their comfort in old age. We can distribute our things to all of these people in order to make their lives a little easier. People who receive these things will respect us for our generosity and will recognize us as a person who reaped *boon*, i.e. merit, from our kindness. And we will feel good. We will feel contentment from our acts of charity.

By giving in these ways, we make the best use of the things we have. Contrast this with the mind that refuses to let go of anything. This tight, stingy state of mind makes it difficult for us to use things even for our own personal benefit. We are reluctant to make use of anything because we worry that nothing will be left. In this case, the very things we work hard to acquire become a source of additional suffering for us, and there is no benefit for others.

As members of a society, we should feel an obligation to help. We all benefited from being members of our society to a greater or lesser extent.

The richness of our lives is reduced by the extent of our refusal to participate in and contribute to our culture. The Buddha taught that, "Eating by oneself is not enjoyable". Find this out for yourself. Eat by yourself. Don't share with anyone else. You will see that it is not a very enjoyable experience. It's easy to see this if we consider a married couple, or even a family, where one person demands everything, while refusing to share with anyone else. How long can this last? If we hog everything the result is that everybody feels miserable, not the least the person who refuses to share.

For example, take an owner of something of value who constantly worries that someone is going to try and snatch his belongings from him. Here we see how someone can struggle to get something of value while, in the end, not deriving any happiness from it. It's as if you bought a fruit but all you get to eat is the peel. If we can come to understand that the things we have can bring us *boon*, we relate to these things in a fresh and wise way. In offering up anything, we shouldn't wait until we have a huge excess of things, or hesitate until we get something that has considerable value before we can let go of single thing.

Worse still would be to keep waiting until death catches us. On the contrary, once we have acquired material things we can offer them up at any time. If we have only a little, we can offer a little. If we have a lot we can offer a lot. Whenever and whatever we have we can offer. If we respond in this way we will certainly reap considerable boon, i.e., the merit that comes from giving. Don't procrastinate until you have such an excess of things that you feel you can now give some of it way. And don't wait until you die and offer things by way of the administrator of your will. I am going on about this because utilizing generosity and unselfishness is an important tactic to reduce the power of the idea of self. This is a matter of letting go in order to reduce the misery that comes with the self-centered focus on *atta* or ego. If you're someone of modest means you can still share your things. But always offer only to the extent of your faith and the sincerity radiating from your Heart. In this way you will always receive happiness from your giving. Your faith and sincerity are the important factors.

It is this energy which produces happiness, not the amount that you offer. If everyone held the peculiar idea that we have to wait until we have a great excess before giving anything at all, every person would suffer from a huge hole in that person's life during the period of acquiring and accumulating this and that.

Under such a circumstance, when a monk or num went out for alms nobody would be there to put food in their bowl. The Buddhist monks and nuns would disappear. Something as seemingly inconsequential as a bit of vegetable, if it is offered to the monk's everyday, will of itself yield benefit to the donor. Clearly, if everyone waits until they have a great surfeit of things, monks, nuns and novices will certainly vanish from the world. In offering something, especially food, that offering sustains the life of another being. In offering food to the monks, nuns, and novices or anyone else we know, that food is intended to help sustain the life of that being. We can call that offering truly "a gift of life".

In the past, there was a legend concerning a man who

gave the "gift of life" by way of sacrificing his life to a starving tigress which was nursing her cubs. Don't misunderstand the implications of this teaching. In no way is it intended to encourage someone to jump off a cliff in front of a tiger in order to offer their flesh and bones. We need our body in order to be able to continue to make offerings and mature in wisdom and compassion. I am elaborating on this so that you can be aware of the principle behind your offerings.

The development of generosity is one of the necessary first steps on the Path to Enlightenment. If you lack the quality of generosity you are lacking something critical in your life.

Though this may be just the first level in your journey, it is certainly of great importance.

The next level concerns maintaining moral precepts. In maintaining the precepts you are refraining from doing evil. For example, you might refrain from killing beings which have sentient life. Both the biggest as well as smallest beings cherish their lives in the same way that we cherish our own lives. When we are ill we run out to find a doctor who can cure our condition because we are so afraid of death. Everybody is afraid of death. Refrain from killing, regardless of whether one does it as a sport or for food.

Have you ever considered that the animal you kill is terrified of losing its life? Some people see animals as just tasty creatures rather than living beings.

This is no different than a tiger eyeing his prey and then pursuing that animal with only the intention of catching and eating it. Someone with a dark mind thinks only of killing something. Don't believe for a moment that this is the mind of a human being! That thought-form is the mind of an animal. The body, the outside form, is that of a human being but the mind is that of an animal. In keeping the moral precepts your mind and your body is that of a human being. Don't feel that I am disparaging you because you might have killed animals in the past. I am underlying the fact that having killed in the past is the catalyst and driving force which initiates killing in the present. Try to refrain from killing, and wait and see if you observe the need for killing to crop up again.

The demand for food doesn't mean that we were born to live and die as monsters. Someone who loves to eat meat has been a kind of monster from the time he was born.

In the north of Thailand, we see that some of the hill tribes who don't eat meat are still able to build their communities and their culture. Instead of meat they eat vegetables, fruits, nuts and seeds. This food gives them plenty of energy.

Rarely do they get ill. They are not affected by skin diseases. People who relish and revel in meat eating have been a kind of monster in the past. It's hard for them to change their diet to restrict meat and keep the precept. Whenever I talk about maintaining the moral precepts I see everyone squirming about feeling guilty concerning their past behavior. Here, I have been talking about the outer layers of our spiritual path. From here we come to the Core.

If we are stable in our precepts, if we have developed

generosity and have the wisdom-based faith that is required to keep us on our spiritual path, our mind will generate *Metta*, or a loving kindness, towards others.

With *Metta* we don't lose sight of the divine significance in the life of all sentient beings. Someone who doesn't keep the precepts just looks to get the blood and flesh of other beings, literally and figuratively.

This kind of person's mind is dark, it is devoid of Metta. Keeping the precepts is a giving gesture which we offer to others. Even though we can kill other beings we stop, we refrain. Even though he can steal things belonging to others, a moral person will always refrain from taking that which doesn't belong to him. This is a kind of offering to others. We are actually acting within the precepts in offering in this subtle way. Therefore, when we hold the precepts, we are also developing generosity at the same time. When we get down to practicing meditation we begin by bringing our mind together with compassion into one object of contemplatation.

Now we are making an offering at a radically and appreciably advanced level. When our minds are calm and abiding in peace there is nothing to create agitation, we can overcome any and all obstacles. When we make our mind calm and peaceful, the craziness of everyday life will evaporate. A primary benefit is the reduction of the power defilements hold over our lives. Anyone who looks after the precepts will see their mind return to the normal-natural state. It won't run around in circles spinning into crazy proliferation. Practicing to make the mind calm and peaceful generates even more *boon* than keeping the precepts. ***

When we practice meditation we enter into the Core. The bark and the cambium of the Path assure that the Core flourishes. This is similar to a tree that has both bark and cambium in order to assure that the Core is strong. The Buddha and all the enlightened beings (arhants) who were the first disciples practiced at the Core and as a result they all became Enlightened.

When one reaches Enlightenment (Nirvana) the idea of the person vanishes never to return again. Everything I have been saying has been an effort to explain in as concise and cogent a manner the foundation of the Buddhist practice in order for you to be able to practice properly.

Do understand that we don't just take one part of the Path and expect to arrive at Nirvana. For instance, don't think that all one must do to become free is to sit in meditation. Or that one just needs to keep the precepts, or develop generosity and sacrifice. The Path isn't about picking and choosing. You have to do it all!

One must methodically proceed through all of the various steps to follow the Buddha's footprints. We pay respects to our mothers and fathers. We pay respects to the monks and nuns. And we chant in praise of the Buddha-Dhamma. And we bring flowers and candles to the temple altar. This is all good in and of itself.

Make your heart pure. Allow your heart to blossom. When we make offerings we feel a kind of bliss inside us. This strengthens and empowers our mind so that we have the energy and courage to face our life challenges. When the mind is immersed in the power of the Buddha-Dhamma we won't be inclined to do anything unskillful.

We have the path of meditation before us, always within us. This is the Path of Practice in the Buddhist religion. If we can't do everything that's necessary such as sitting in meditation, holding to the precepts, developing generosity we can still show respect to the Buddha, to our parents, and to the monks and nuns. Do whatever you can and the Path will open before you. Make your heart a Heart of compassion towards your relatives. Open your heart wide towards your friends.

Develop these qualities in yourself to the utmost in order to keep inclining towards the Buddha-Dhamma. If you don't have these virtues you are not far removed from the animal realm. Consider the animal; it eats then it sleeps, then it goes out to eat again. Eating and sleeping while waiting for death to arrive. The class of animals one step higher in the chain of evolution eats sleeps and also works. These animals are the farm animals we know. When the *sleep-eat* animal dies, the people typically devour its flesh. The draught animal that eats, sleeps, and works, therefore dies without meaning.

Many people live like this too, merely eating, sleeping and working. Actually, they are only subsisting like animals. Such people die like animals because they have done nothing to uplift themselves during their lifetimes. This is just eating to live while waiting to die.

What value is there to merely being born, then eating and sleeping whilst awaiting death?

Someone using a farm animal to plow their fields doesn't see the value of that animal. They just exploit that animal for their work. When the animal dies the owner immediately becomes pleased because now he can eat the animal, use its hide and sell some of the meat in the market. The owner doesn't feel a touch of compassion for the animal. Someone who acts unskillfully and doesn't do any good at all when he or she is alive will be re-born as an animal.

But if that person, following my instructions diligently practices meditation, they can be guaranteed that they will not be re-born as an animal. If we are generous, hold to the precepts, and practice meditation to the point where the mind is powerful and courageous, we can reach Nirvana.

And that's that.

An Enlightened person will not be born again. They won't have to be born into this confusion and chaos again. Everything I have been pointing to is the basic foundation of Buddhism. I ask you to remember this teaching and go on the Path of Purification. Follow this Path and your life will certainly mature and become more and more meaningful.

Bringing the Forest into the Heart—And the Heart into the World

When the body dies, disintegrating line with the nature of its various elements of earth, air, fire and water, the mind will keep on rolling. If the dictating adverse conditions of unawareness, craving, attachment and karma are still present there will be a rebirth. The defilements which block Enlightenment plus karma necessitate this arising. As long as the defilements remain in the system they will produce the momentum leading into a form or formless realm.

Because of our karmic inheritance we have to reappear in some world which is built into the illusion (Samsara). This is one of the worlds in the Samsara-wat. Once born into this plane there is only aging, illness and death ahead of us. As these conditions manifest we stew in a pot of unsatisfactoriness and suffering. This is the plight of an ignorant, fear-ridden creature. Here in this plane of existence we are trapped in the inescapable cycle of birthing, aging, getting ill and dying. We experience all varieties of pleasure and pain as we pursue a myriad of strategies to extricate ourselves from the relentless suffering.

We put these strategies into operation in order to allow us to be who-we-think-we-are while attempting to extricate ourselves from suffering. Invariably, we find this a hopeless endeavor that takes us back into the re-birthing cycle again and again. In fact, most of the world is populated with hopeless beings in hopeless situations.

They don't have even a sliver of a chance to live a more refined and evolved life or to break away from this cycle of re-birthing. Once more, one more birth in a long drawn out saga. Here we are, again.

Ignorance, greed, attachment and the karma making mechanism are the factors which instigate the birthing catastrophe. We must first purify our behavior we must put a stop to it. As long as you are not pure in keeping the precepts, you won't be prepared and ready to enter the Path to Enlightenment. If they are pure you can precede with confidence to the do the necessary work.

The Noble Eightfold Path and the Three Teachings are at the heart of Buddhism - essentially never doing any evil, refining goodness to the point of elegance. Engaging in this process makes the mind stable. What comes of this process is the utterly unshakeable mind. Not doing evil purifies the mind, bringing goodness to completion. So, the purification of one's speech and actions, known as moral trainings, are the critical factors at the first level of mental cultivation (Bhavana). It has been the result of the karma-making factor which keeps beings spinning on the wheel of becoming. This is why this training is right at the very beginning of the holy life.

The development of Insight is possible because good intentions itself opens doors. Just working with that energy will place us in a position to learn, will stimulate the evolutionary process-even if we are a bit off the most direct path. When someone practices with good intentions the mind will be quick to learn, enhancing their already active wisdom in order to control the body and to keep it from engaging in foolish activities. Of special importance is the wisdom functioning as a sentry to protect the mouth from speaking in an unskillful manner. So, here we see that wisdom is a necessary adjunct every step of the way. We rely on wisdom to purify our behavior, to stabilize concentration and to deepen and broaden wisdom itself.

With morality established we could then begin to calm the mind with Samadhti or tranquility practice. When the mind is adept at concentration and absorption it will have enough strength to suppress the five hindrances. This opens the door for wisdom to naturally arise. We train the mind to develop concentration (Samadhti) and absorption (Jhana) through the practice of tranquility meditation. Meditation requires effort-not just any effort but *proper effort* which you are willing and capable of sustaining.

Our effort provides the most benefit when it is directed at letting go or abandoning. We come into the practice with the willingness to abandon, to accept relinquishment, to die. Abandoning lightens the mind and makes you feel unburdened. When you abandon your unskillful tendencies you will experience that an onerous burden has finally dropped. What is to be abandoned? It is the proliferations on the past and future. What is to be nurtured is sustained attention on the present moment. The past and future can be abandoned by simply not giving them any attention. These realms don't like to be snubbed. When the past and future are disregarded, they lose their power to imprison our life. To put it more expressively, the past and future will feel somewhat offended and hand over your life to the present.

We have become habituated to living in the past and future. The past is, after all, our history, which we gather and make into our identity. Stop doing this! You are embarking on a futile endeavor if you think you will learn from the past, resolve all your problems, understand your family, connect some fragmentary thoughts and images to a forgotten experience, etc. Your memory is a liar. Let go of the past and you are free to be in the present. The real insights you need to come to understand are right in the present moment. They are right here and now.

As for the future, people spend much of there life energy engineering and constructing a future world according to their wishes. It's all wishful thinking with only an unreal past to substantiate it. To imagine the future as it actually will be is hopeless. All the present moments between here and the image of a future-to-be affects the form reality will take. The past, which we really should discard is, in fact, that which fabricates the same kind of situations and conflicts that are all too familiar to us.

So, keep your meditation right in the present moment, to the point where you don't even know what time it is, don't even know if it is morning or evening. You don't really care. You know only the present. This needs to be developed through what the Masters called *skillful-means*. You live awake in the now without tossing away your karmic responsibilities.

We have to circumvent the rolling commentary and chatter which expresses rational thinking in order to abide in the present moment. This is similar to the 24 hour news channels running the same story over and over, again and again adding a bit of embellishment. Wisdom recognizes the problems that come from listening and following the inner dialogue that is thought. We need to learn to pull the plug on the notion that thinking is something to cherish. Today I will offer you two effective ways to do this.

The first skillful-means that I recommend is to observe every mind moment so closely that there isn't the opportunity for thought to intrude. The meditator stays continuously connected to a particular meditation object. The second skillful-means requires that we turn our attention to the space between thought. The space between thought is silence. This is a particularly effective practice in an office environment. *Silence imbues the mind with the capability to concentrate and thereby, slip out from under distraction*

Wisdom with its wider, deeper perspective sees the limitation and problems associated with thought. Those moments when wisdom is functioning are mind-moments that strengthen the mind. As we become established in silence, wisdom sees to it that we maintain the appropriate relationship to silence and thought. Recognizing the *feeling* of silence is a priority. In the case of attending to silence, it inclines the mind in that direction.

In the case of thinking, it consents to allow cogitating only when there is a real need to think. Such as the times when I need to consider and evaluate a matter within time and space (embedded aspects of thought) and centers around conventional reality. "What school would be best for my child?" "When should I take my vacation?" "What food should I eat to meet the requirements of my body?"

In Buddhist practice, the intention in developing tranquility (concentration and absorption) is to gather one's mental energies into a single point and to make that single point solid and resilient. This is called *ekkatada* - the basis for cultivating the mind Beyond-the-Known.

The mind must be trained by progressing through inward

stages, as it inclines deeper into the holy life. There is an amplification of spiritual energy. This may be realized by listening to the explanations of those who are already skilled, by being determined to practice in line with those explanations, then by actually doing it.

Many people drop out of a meditative practice because they don't have the proper principles to guide them. They miss the Path, tending instead to stumble into the blind spots and presumptions they harbor in their character.

In practice, first, we investigate and explore cause and effect exclusively within the bounds of the body, i.e. 'What is this body of mine made of? How does it come about so that its parts are complete, functional and synchronous and thus, able to perform its duties admirably? What is it to be used for? What keeps it going? Is it fate to develop or to deteriorate? Is it really mine? Who am I?

Then turning to mental phenomenon-Do greed, anger, delusion, love, hatred, etc., arise at the body or at the mind? What do they come from? Where do they come from? When they arise are they pleasant or stressful? This investigation demands present-moment mindfulness. This investigation is a stage in training the mind. It is an investigation into remembering what we have forgotten. It is a looking into the nature of things, probing and forcing inquiry into the mental proliferating which defines the crazy mind. The ridiculous, insidious progress from thought to attachment to self-concern describes the chain that sets up and habituates unskillful thought formations.

Investigation is the way of scientists and philosophers, as well. We are sensitive, intellectually endowed beings who are living lives which afford this opportunity. We are not toiling fields in a drought plagued environment, or working in a sweat-shop in India for example.

When Samadhti is still embryonic and weak it won't have the horsepower to explore and investigate things in line with the causes and effects that actually arise from the mind in the present. Generally people are working with around 100-150 c.c.'s of mental energy which is enough to get around, to assemble a child's bicycle, and the like.

Let us begin by positioning ourselves into the first phase of genuine, effective practice. So, following the instruction from the Buddha we focus on one spot, solidly into one object *(ekkakata)*. Our intention must be to gather together the mind preventing it from spreading out its treasury of energies into everywhere and nowhere. Turn your attention to just *one thing*. That one thing can be the experience of breathing, the idea of loving kindness, or on one location such as one organ of the body, etc.

Next I will talk about focusing on the present moment awareness of the breath. Ask yourself, "Am I breathing in or out"? "Is the breath long or short? Is there a point where the breath pauses?

That which **knows** the answers is the next, more refined object of awareness. If you can be with this for 50-60 breaths you will have attained sustained attention on the breath. Remember as you develop this, if you can do this for just one cycle that implies you can do it indefinitely. This is natural law.

Once the mind is adept at maintaining a steady focus, we can then develop clear insight (*Vipassana*) based on an understanding of the three characteristics; annica, dukkha, and annatta.

This where we gain pure knowledge and vision of things as they actually are, thus reaching toward release from all things detrimental and defiling. ****

When the mind has attained strength from this solidifying of energies it is already able to uproot attachments ---- mistaken presuppositions---and to cleanse the mind so that , at least momentarily, it is bright and clear. You will certainly experience a profound sense of well being. Perhaps meditative knowledge of one sort or another will arise in the moment. Meditative knowledge is often perceived as a remarkable or strange phenomenon since it arises in a form not associated with mental imaginings (at the subjective thought level), but from the emanation of the inherent truth acting in the present in away that you have never experienced. When you come upon it, inevitably you will say to yourself with a sense of deep satisfaction and relief, "So, that's how it is!"

Touching this Truth occurs without strain. To BE with the energy at the Heart (the non-condition referred to as "Is-ness") doesn't bring about fatigue or debilitate your mental capacity. Its presence refines your mind and behavior in a way that impresses and inspires others, attracting them to who you've become. Regardless of that "by product", stay right on the job, consistently and constantly maintaining vigilance over the mind. As the momentum of your practice continues, your mindfulness will stabilize. At the very least you will experience a pervading, encompassing sense of peace and well-being in proportion to the extent of your own individual practice attainments and the magnitude of your confidence.

Don't let feelings of greed, desire, disappointment, anxiety or fear intrude on this mental state. These sinister forces have great power and emerge in practice in deceptive ways that try to lure you into forgetting or retreating from attentiveness. Strive to maintain the attitude of trust and conviction that accompanies faith.

If things are not coming together, switch the practice to focusing on an aspect of the body such as the bones or some internal organ with an inclination to take particular notice of the repulsive nature of the specific organ. In the Pali scriptures this is known as *asuba gumatahn*. It is a practice which will ground you, bring sobriety to the mind and go a long way to re-balance your excessive fascination with attractive forms (See this in the standpoint that we are already drunk on family relationships as well as our fondness for intimate sensual relationships. Additionally we are at least somewhat intoxicated by the Internet, concept cars, games, fashion, electronic gadgets and the like as well). Surprisingly and even ironically, focusing on the unattractive aspects of the sentient beings we have a partiality for is a practice that leads to sublime peacefulness.

A subtle, yet simple way to develop this practice is to begin by focusing the mind on bare awareness itself. The nature of awareness is that it is always seen against the backdrop of the mind. Or is it vice-versa? Have a look. The mind is like the wind, if the wind doesn't come into contact with anything, you won't know there is such a thing. Varieties of insanity can be seen from this level of understanding.

At the conventional level there must be something in front to sense there is something behind. We can't write upon nothing. Accept whatever you get from your practice. The results depend upon many factors. As you know from your life experience in the world, effort, determination and karma play important roles in everything we pursue. Laziness is the one penchant that traps most people. It can be countered with wisdom-based faith and authentic, intense determination.

In focusing, examine the object in line with the principles of the foundations of mindfulness *satipatthana*. In other words, sort out the body's various aspects until you can see "This isn't me, this isn't my Self".

This sort of focused examination which gives rise to this realization can be done in two ways:

When focused on the target, don't give any thought to what the target is or who is focusing. Let there simply be awareness and the act of focusing. Do not name, label or think about the target, the thing you are directed towards. Let there be simply the sense of being with the object.

Or when focused exclusively on the target, at the same time stay aware that, "This is the target of the mind. This is the mind examining an object. This is mindfulness (*sati*)". This is astute wisdom which is sees into the Truth of the object being considered. All the while you stand back from everything arising and passing away adding nothing personal into the relationship.

This second method is perhaps best suited for those who are sensitive and experienced. Both methods, give rise to Samadhti and Wisdom-Compassion.

Of paramount importance is not to do want anything

from the practice. Desire is toxic. Desire breeds fear. Both cause restlessness and anxiety and pull you out of the present time (no-time). Use your mental energy to investigate the approach you've used to bring the mind into the object, how you maintained mindfulness, and what resulted from this interface. You are teaching your "Dhamma-intending" mind what is what. Again, I caution you to be careful to avoid desire and fear as best as you can. They will certainly push you out of the present. **And, the continuity of "present-ness" generates the momentum that generates evolution.** Your learning to see how the mind behaves in order to see what pulls it out of its highest, most refined mode---the wisdom-compassion passage way.

Observation and investigation are critical to the development of Insight (Wisdom-Compassion). The meditator must observe how the mind behaves under training within the context of two occasions: 1) present moment and 2) after withdrawal. Some will be able to do that when the mind is gathered and absorbed in one-pointed-ness. Others will do this only after the mind has withdrawn and has been released into some brief moments of stillness. Sometimes, and for some meditators, *Insight* that they have garnered comes only after the fact. In the momentary stillness that arises, retrospective reflections and deliberation can reveal the process that has occurred.

While you are exerting effort in training the mind, a *strange and wonderful* phenomenon may occur on its own. The mind will, on its own, withdraw from its external objects and gather into a whole, letting go of all labels and attachments dealing with past or future. There will simply be bare awareness paired with its very positive obsession with the present as it is. This feels like *really* being alive for *real*. This is nothing like the dull, resigned acceptance we regard as normal. There will be no duality arising from space or time. No inside, no outside no future and no past. In this moment there is only Heart. The mind has entered (or you might say, merged) into the Heart. The mind has reverted to normality.

Life as we know it is still going on, but there is likely to be no reference to time and so there certainly cannot be any attachment to the body (which necessarily hinges on awareness of the past and/or the future). The mind has righted itself. The mind has gone inward to know only itself as its own object of awareness.

This is called the *bhavacitta* (something like the underlying hum of a computer engaged with itself and not involved with software). The mind is in the mind (bhavanga, the underlying essence of mind "where" the mind reverts to between its responses to stimuli). The *bhavanga* state is the abiding of the ordinary, uncreative consciousness.

Though one may think that this transformation of consciousness signifies Enlightenment, this is not the case. For the mind-in-the-mind still contains a template of the five aggregates, the five casually conditioned elements of existence viz.; corporeality, form, feeling, perception, mental formations and consciousness represented within this state of being. That implies vulnerability to birth and becoming. That is, this energy can give rise to continued birth in the future.

This phenomenon is similar to what happens when one falls off into a vivid state of dream consciousness. The difference depends upon how strength of one present-ness, one's self-awareness. As this phenomenon arises, those who are collected and discerning will be aware of what is happening. There will be an acknowledgement of what occurred and what is present without getting either excited or fretful. However, those whose mindfulness is still weak and whose characters tend to be gullible will lapse into a dream-like state. When they come out of this they are likely to be confused by the visions they encountered. Further training will provide access to these natural conditions as they actually are. One needs only to move up another notch along the way.

This amazing phenomenon of itself and on its own, doesn't lead towards wisdom. However, it can be seen as a step up to a higher rung on the ladder. Here I am trying to use language where language is severely limited. We can just say that this is a preliminary stage in training the mind. It can suppress the five hindrances while giving rise to a sense of peace and well being for the duration of the experience. Because the hindrances are suppressed and one abides in peace, this strengthens the mind, makes it more confident, and leads toward further development.

These visions happen to some people and for others they don't occur at all. They are useful only when they are seen for what they are, a seductive illusion. Therefore, a proficient meditator will have the capability to see right through them. They can be used as a peaceful abiding, for they have value in this way. They are most useful (having the least downside) for those with incisive intelligence. They are a detriment to the practice for someone who clings to them, or takes them personally. This kind of practitioner can get lost in fascination and lose the critical foundation supporting conventional reality.

Should people who are prone to conceit and arrogance encounter these kinds of visions they tend to believe that they are something unique and that they are very special people to have encountered them (reinforcing their ego). It is hard to dislodge them from this perspective. The end result can be that the practitioner has to face even more obstructive circumstances. This situation, we might describe, as hard-core clinging. Generally, the Masters point out the danger and caution meditators to be careful with signs and visions and to ignore them should they manifest.

Along the Path there will always be interesting and fascinating phenomena which the meditator will come upon. Recognize that regardless of whether visions and signs arise, they are not what we are seeking through practice. When seen with acute discernment they are revealed as defilements, clouding discernment and a principle obstruction to the development of insight.

We are practicing to let go of all defilements, all of the five hindrances; sensual desire, ill will, torpor-lethargy, restlessness-anxiety, and doubt. And then to examine the 5 aggregates (*khandha*) with sharp focus and perspicacity so that they can be seen for what they are. When seen deeply, the meditator will naturally become disenchanted with them. He or she will lose their fascination for them, and they will gladly let go of them-never to enter into and grasp a hold of them again.

When we have developed Samadhti that is strong enough to keep at bay or suppress the five hindrances we can move on into the phase of practice which emphasizes Insight or Vipassana.

Insight, beyond the superficial and insignificant, can only arise when concentration is strong enough to support discovery. Insight will then arise as we develop Samadhti. That is why the two cannot really be separated from one another. Insight does arise simultaneously when our inherent intelligence is able to see the primary and most obvious fact of life--- that all conditioned things (*sankhara*) arise and pass away. These things don't belong to anyone. They belong to Nature. They are conditions. Nature has no issue with them. When unenlightened beings play and interact with them, clinging to them, they then become a source of suffering. Wisdom arises concurrently with awareness of change (*Annica*). It also arises when awareness lights upon the inherent fact that suffering (*Dukkha*) is hard wired, and the most uncomfortable fact of all, that there is ultimately and really there is no one here (*Annatta*).

With the realization of the fact of change, suffering and non-self embedded in the mind, the mind will become disenchanted and dispassionate with regard to conditioned things.

The Insight arises that conditioned things coupled with our involvement with them is the cause of our unhappiness. The mind will not dare move onto anything. It will dwell in a state of matured and chastened dispassion. This Insight is rooted in tranquility. This is the essence of Vipassana Insight. This is that which sees deeply into the nature of all conditioned phenomena and is able to uproot attachments to physical and mental phenomena of every sort. That is the point of the whole enterprise known as Vipassana.

There is more than can be understood. Insight or Wisdom

is the light of knowledge, or Real-ization (seeing the Real). Seeing into the truth of all natural conditions (*Sabhava-Dhamma*) together with the cause for their arising and passing away. A mind that has reached this level should be employed into the service of coming to the Truth-as-it-is. And, from that point, the whole mess winds down.

Should insight still be weak, a skillful tact is to return to Samadhti practice in order to firmly establish the mind in one-pointed tranquility (*ekkakata*). Then, select a part of the body such as the bones, or hair or teeth or intestines as your object of contemplation.

Or, you can probe into a question occupying your thoughts. (Such as the questions that were highlighted in the book "Questions from the City, Answers from the Forest"). Whether you take something that is pressing on your mind or a part of the body, examine what you have before you to see if it is a stable, permanent entity.

Is there is something in any body part that can offer real happiness? Is there is something about your concerns that holds any hope that you will taste supreme happiness? Is there anything about your well-thought-out curiosity that smacks of ultimate reality? Or, does all of it fall within the parameters of the three characteristics of change, unsatisfactoriness and non-self? See for yourself.

The Truth is that all conditions and things simply arise from their causes; unawareness, desire, attachment and karma. They are not at all personal---to emphasize, they are *not* at all personal. They fall under the three characteristics I have mentioned; change, unsatisfactoriness and non-self. They dissolve on their own into the cauldron of infinite varieties of potential phenomenon in line with the momentum of energy known as karma.

The body we are using will disband when that which it is depends upon is exhausted. That is for sure. The body as a dependent formation executing and operating, in one way or another, has no meaning at all. As I have said, it is merely functioning.

When you utilize the power of the concentrated mind, you will see with Insight the way-things-are. You will discover, through *real*-ization (uncovering the real which has been blocked by ignorance) the cause and effect principle of all phenomenon. The mind will never again be deluded into becoming attached, enchanted, and caught in liking or disliking. There will be equanimity established upon a base of wisdom.

Earlier I warned you about amazing phenomena that can arise. The meditator should be aware of *visions and signs* which, for some meditators, arise when the mind gathers and all the vagrant energies in the mind are drawn together.

Visions and signs can arise in the development of one's Samadhi practice. When they arise, they arise in a different way for different practitioners.

Sometimes a vision will arise when the practitioner considers his or her own body or body part. He/she will see the body or body part as utterly foul, and in a state of shocking decomposition. He or she may be looking down on body as a pile of ashes or a skeleton lying supine.

A meditator can go overboard here and feel such revulsion for the body that they attempt to kill it. In other cases, visions may be benign and pleasant such as when visions of divine beings arise. Or they may be frightening as with the vision of some sort of creature from the hungry realms.

One typical phenomenon is the *preta*. The preta is a disembodied being with a long, long neck, tiny mouth and huge stomach. Psychologically, the preta is associated with addiction.

As for the characteristics of a sign, the constituents tend to be more obscure. A whispering voice may be heard, it may be a voice of someone we respect telling instructing us to examine a particular truth, or beware of a coming event. Or, it may be the voice of an enemy who is up to some kind of mischief, appearing to us just before it will come to do us harm.

On the other hand, another sign may involve a person who means us well. There may be an unidentified voice appearing, elucidating a truth which is thought-provoking and worth of consideration. Meditators often call these occasions to be teachings and warnings from the Dhamma. Take notice of how all these strange occurrences indicate how the mental currents of different individuals can impinge on one another. You will find this to be quite an interesting contemplation.

Visions and signs are part of the meditation mindscape. When they appear, they appear in a flash - a lightening brief moment. They arise from the power of mundane *jhana* and are composed of a great accumulation of mental concocting and attachment. The swirl of energy which comes from concocting and attachment, sustain and instill them with a sense of reality. Whether they arise or not depends upon karma and individual character tendencies. Actually, they should be seen as a vexation to the concentrated mind. Visions and signs can get out of hand to someone who has a gullible nature and doesn't give much thought to what is reasonable. They tend to escalate quickly and to grow all out of bounds, to the point where one can lose all one's bearings. Once attached to these phenomena, the meditator can lose all perspective on reality. They become spellbound. Thus, visions or signs are things to be treated with caution.

If you get caught in the fascination of a vision which has attached to you, you should regard it as an enemy. You are obliged to discover a tactic to combat its potential to unhinge your mind. Try to extricate yourself from it by doing heavy, tiring work until the body is exhausted and weary. That will focus attention on the body and bring us down to the earth. Or, bring up sensual memories and indulge in them. The interest and delight that is manufactured from these memory clips will override the vision. Or, as a last resort, do something that will seem to put your life at risk - jump into a barrel of water and stay under to the limits of your courage. That will frighten away the attached vision. If you are mentoring a trainee, you can provoke him/her to furious anger (such as suggesting that they are lying about their states of conscious; that they are untrustworthy and unworthy; that they intend to use the benefits of their practice in dark ways, etc.) and the vision or sign will immediately disappear in the passion of their wrath

The mode of consciousness which specifically gives rise to Wisdom-Compassion is called"*Upacara Samadhti*".

Upacara Samadhti is often referred to as threshold

Samadhti as it is that status which is right on the verge of entering transcendence "*Appana Samadhti*"

When using the breath as the meditation object, Upacara Samadhti arises when the mind has gathered into one spot at the breath point. The mind has withdrawn from external proliferations and concerns, and gathered itself through absorption into just that spot in the mind. However, it is yet to break free from sensing, thinking, feeling, and considering/contemplating. The mind is trying to let go of the last vestige of its connection to the now quite refined breath point. When it refines a wee bit further, it will enter Appana Samadhti; transcendent Samadhti.

The meditator who has been working with the in-and-out breath as their meditation object will be amalgamating all their mental energy on the arising and falling away. Just the falling away segment is quite sufficient. As the factors underpinning concentration deepen the mind becomes more and more refined letting go of its preoccupations and inclining deeper into the object.

When the mind has let go of that last vestige of attachment, that one point, as a point, will disappear. The stilling of the in-and-out breath indicates this state has been attained. When there is no sensation of the in-and-out breath, the mind's attention becomes fully absorbed into the breath.

One's attention has expanded to incorporate every bit of the breath. The mind will have slipped into Appana. When Appana Samadhti has arisen the mind is no longer grasping or binding to the meditation point. You know the breath from the initial nano-second of inhalation, through the inhalation phase, back down the exhalation to the pause point, and then into the next cycle.

The object disappears and there is simply, we can say, awareness of awareness. The mind is attending to what is at the Heart of the experience of awareness of the breath; peace. Mindfulness is still and absolutely full. "You" cannot attain this stage of peace...it is the mind that attains it as the notion of self peels away. Without effort, the mind has entered the mind. There is only peace. The world has been left behind.

When meditators are in this state, they are unable to investigate Dhamma because there is no context or no duality to work with. The primary benefit of entering into this state and magnitude of profound concentration is that it will   vanquish mental effluents (*asava*) over time.

When the causes that yield authenticate Appana withdraw, the mind drops back into Upacara Samadhti from where the meditator is able to consider objects of Dhamma, and the cause and effect relationship from which discernment can arise. It comes back into Upacara Samadhti imbued with the energy of Appana Samadhti".

These natural processes show that mundane-worldly phenomena are the raw material for transcendent phenomena (supra-phenomenon). When we see with the eye of wisdom that all worldly phenomenon generates suffering, that it is all in a state of change, and that none of it can create happiness for that which-we-think-we-are, we become disenchanted with them. We can now see that they are dangerously delusive, and then drop them like a hot potato.   The greatest danger in clutching to them is that they pull us down into darker, heavier realms.

Any sensitive being can get a perspective on the human predicament and the possibility of transcending it. If they are able to see things in this way, as they are, they should prioritize intelligently and willingly put their life on the line to escape the danger, conflict and suffering that there present situation is causing them. They would endeavor to reset their attitude to establish a proper view, which supports the factors that light up the Path. They will attempt to use everything they can make use of (that is everything) to cut off, to drop, to shake off their attachments to worldly phenomenon including mundane happiness and that which is involved in the knowing of these things. Ultimately there is no agent attaining or getting anything. Natural phenomenon arises and passes away of its own.

When the fruit of practice is ripened, the meditator can see that freedom from attachment and freedom from belief that the conventional world is an appropriate refuge for human beings and that the little bit of ephemeral so-called happiness that can be snatched from the world is unworthy of our inherent *nobility*. That person rises above the realm of the ordinary person. That person transcends the insanity of unawareness, that person becomes a real human being-a *spiritual* Being. This is where the world ends. This is where you come to the freedom that has been waiting for you

Ajahn Sumano Bhikkhu

Acknowledgement

I would like to thank the following for their participation and contributions to this book.

Benjasiri Suebsiri
Chavit and Saranya Chindavanig
Eddy Sutton and Associates
Jindtaraht, Yongyoot, Dang, and Lek
Jinin Trakansuebkun
Jueng Panawayt
Judtharat Ua Umnooy
Karan Pipitsombat
Keith and Wan Bell
Khao Yai Garden Lodge Family
Mac and Sandy McClintic
Nipon Pinsrisrat
Orathai Kiatvarangkura
Polachao Nopavong Na Ayudhaya
Punjapol Saneahsangkom
Ratnakumar Duraisingn
Rutchina Pongpladisai
Siriyong, Sayan (Oy), Mo and Mueo
Sriratana Chouvuttisatien
Suwapa Sookkah
Teh Choo Keong
The Klincajohn Family
The Pongphanrada Family
Woranit Chaiyaharn

Special Thanks:
Ajahn Kanakorn for computer backup and Technical Help

I would also like to thank all my other friends, too numerous to mention, without whose participation and sacrifices this book would not have been possible.